D1752292

Pocket Bushtucker

Peter Latz

jukurrpa books

A jukurrpa book, first published in 1999 by
IAD Press
PO Box 2531
Alice Springs
NT   0871
Phone   (08) 8951 1334
Fax   (08) 8952 2527
email: iadpress@ozemail.com.au

Copyright © Peter Latz 1999

This book is copyright. Apart from any fair dealing for the purposes of private study, research, criticism or review, as permitted under the Copyright Act, no part may be reproduced by any process without written permission. Please forward all inquiries to IAD Press at the above address.

National Library of Australia Cataloguing-in-Publication data:

Latz, P. K. (Peter Kenneth)
Pocket bushtucker: a field guide to the plants of Central Australia and their traditional uses.

Includes index.
ISBN 1 86465 023 0.

1. Aborigines, Australian - Australia, Central - Food. 2. Aborigines, Australian - Australia, Central - Medicine. 3. Aborigines, Australian - Australia, Central - Ethnobotany. 4. Wild foods - Australia, Central. 5.Wild plants, Edible - Australia, Central. 6. Medicinal plants - Australia, Central. I. Green, Jenny. II. Title

581.6309942

Design: Brenda Thornley
Illustrations: Jenny Green
Additional drawings: Brenda Thornley, Felicity Green, Daphne Cotton, Julie Jones, Stephanie Mackie-Schneider, Christine Bruderlin, Milton Andrews
Photos: Peter Latz
Map: Brenda Thornley
Printed in Australia by Gillingham Printers, Adelaide

CONTENTS

Publisher's Note	iv
Acknowledgments	iv
Introduction	1
Map of the Area Covered in this Book	10
Central Australian Aboriginal Languages	12
Grasses and Sedges	15
Herbs	33
Sub-shrubs	63
Shrubs	79
Trees	149
Vines, Parasites and Fungi	187
Glossary	206
Cross Reference of Plant Names	208

PUBLISHER'S NOTE
- This field guide is a companion to the IAD Press publication *Bushfires & Bushtucker*. Much of the specific plant information from that book has been presented here in a condensed form, but readers should refer to it for more detail.
- **As there are more than 2000 plant species in Central Australia, neither this book nor the larger volume is intended to be a comprehensive listing.** The plants identified here have been selected as the most widely seen and most used of the many hundreds to be found in the area.
- *Pocket Bushtucker* covers a limited geographical area, and you will find frequent references to it in the text: for example, a plant might be found 'throughout the area' or 'in the northern third of the area'. For details, refer to the map on p. 10.
- Many of the Aboriginal plant names and some scientific names have been updated for this edition. New botanical and linguistic information is constantly arising, and these revisions should not be seen as the last word on either subject.
- The section headings used in *Pocket Bushtucker* are intended as handy labels rather than strict classifications. The question, for example, of whether the mallee is a tree or a shrub could be debated at some length; and indeed some members of staff at Jukurrpa Books would say that it has been. In the end, we have tried to place the entries where we think people will look first.

ACKNOWLEDGMENTS
Thanks to:
Jenny Green and Myf Turpin (Central Australian Dictionaries Program), Robert Hoogenraad, David Nash and Craig Martin for revisions to the Aboriginal plant names.
Also Hilda Pwerl, Gracie Mpetyan, Rosie Mpetyan, Tommy Thompson, Amy Ngampwerle, Mary Thompson, Janie Mpetyane, Blanche Ross, Alison Ross, Jacob Peltharre, Peter Young, Glory Ngal, Rita Ngal, Rosie Ngal, Kitty Peltharr (Anmatyerr and Kaytetye speakers who assisted with updating language material).
Dave Albrecht (NT Parks and Wildlife Commission) for botanical information.
Mike Gillam for the cover photo.

INTRODUCTION

PLANTS USED FOR FOOD

A casual visitor to Central Australia, glancing out of their car window or walking through the bush, would find it hard to imagine that there is a wide variety of plant foods available in the desert environment, especially during a drought when what plants are present appear withered or dead. It is during these periods of drought that Aboriginal people's ingenuity has been taxed to the utmost. Through their intimate knowledge of the resources available from the land, however, they have been able to obtain enough food to satisfy their needs; and at least 140 different plant species are still utilised as food in the Centre.

Fruits

Non-Aboriginal people are generally not very impressed with desert fruits. Reared on a diet of large, sweet fruit, produced by grossly overbred, unnatural plants, they usually consider desert fruits small, lacking in flavour and rarely worth the effort of collecting. What they don't consider is that these fruits are at least as nutritious as those they eat, and that the bush plants do not require extensive nurturing.

Fruits are important to Central Australia's Aboriginal people, but although they are a good source of certain minerals and vitamins, their calorific value is relatively low. Most fruits are only available for a short period of the year and they often spoil quickly. There is also the problem of competition from other animals, including insects. On the other hand, these animals (usually birds such as emus but also, surprisingly enough, dingoes) take a while to reach large numbers after droughts, and in the interim period generous amounts of fruit are available. When they do reach high numbers and consume most of the fruit, they themselves are then easily caught and eaten.

Some desert plants also produce fruit which keep well and are therefore available for a long time after they are first produced, whereas in non-desert environments, the higher density of fruit-eating animals means that the fruit are generally consumed by them as soon as they ripen. The dry climate also ensures that fruits are less likely to rot and thus will be available for longer periods.

Seeds

A plant whose seeds are readily eaten by animals is at an evolutionary disadvantage, so most plants ensure that their seeds are protected from animal predation in some way. Some seeds are bitter, others have a hard coating of some sort and still others are very small and cryptic. Anyone utilising these seeds must spend a considerable amount of effort in gathering and treating them before they can be eaten. But seeds can still be an important food source. Not only do they usually have a high calorific value but they are often a rich source of proteins, oils, vitamins and fibre.

An important characteristic of many desert plants is their prolific seed production. The seeds may be small, but they can often be collected in large numbers and for this reason are an important part of the traditional diet.

Tubers and other underground foods

Because most fruits and seeds are available only during periods of flush growth, tubers and bulbs, being available even during the worst droughts, are of great importance. They are hidden away under the ground, however, and considerable skill is required to first find and then obtain reasonable quantities without expending a great deal of energy.

Although the nutritional value of these starchy foods is limited, the high water content of at least one of the tubers made it important, in the past, to certain Aboriginal people. During cooler months this source of water was sufficient to allow them to occupy waterless areas, sometimes for several months at a time.

Greens

This loose category generally includes plants which supply edible leaves, buds and shoots, although in some cases flowers and pods can also be eaten. None of the 13 or so species used is important in the traditional diet, other than for short periods. This is not surprising as they are generally not very palatable and are low in calories. Greens are generally only consumed in any quantity immediately after the first rains following a dry period, a time when there are few other plant foods available.

Honey

One of the characteristics of the species *Homo sapiens* is

our particular craving for sweet foods, and Aboriginal people of the Centre are no exception. Sweet foods are rare in the desert and for this reason they are one of the most sought-after foods — to the extent that often more energy is expended in obtaining the food than is supplied by the food itself.

Most honey is obtained either from native beehives or from the swollen abdomen of the honeyant, and although the honey stored by these insects is obtained from plants, it is better classed as an animal food.

Honey is obtained directly in various ways from the flowers of about 15 plant species. Flowers from the *Grevillea* plants are sucked to get at the honey; flowers from other species, including some of the eucalypts, contain less honey and are generally plucked from the tree and soaked in water. The sweetened water is then drunk; no doubt the insects that are inadvertently mixed in this liquid supply additional nutrients. Occasionally the honey in some flowers becomes fermented and a slightly alcoholic drink is produced.

Edible grubs and caterpillars

The majority of non-Aboriginal people blanch at the very thought of eating insects, thereby depriving themselves of an important and delicious food source. Insects, as a general rule, are richer in protein, fats and minerals than most other animal foods and are considered to be delicacies in many cultures.

Grubs and caterpillars are of course not plant foods but they are included in this book because they are so closely associated with specific plants. At least 24 Central Australian plant species harbour edible grubs and caterpillars. Most of these insects are moth larvae which spend most of their life boring into the roots and trunks of certain plants, but several caterpillars which feed on leaves are also eaten.

Sap-sucking insects

These are small sucking insects which feed exclusively on plant saps. After they have extracted the nutrients required for their growth from this sap they excrete the remainder as a sugary substance. This could be considered to be a 'dessert' food, in demand because of its somewhat sweet taste, but certainly not one of the most nutritious foods available.

One of the major advantages of this food source is its availability when other plant foods are scarce. Lerp scales, at least those on the river red gum, are often available during dry periods and in fact they are unavailable during wet periods as heavy rain washes them off the leaves.

Insect galls

Although only two forms of insect galls are commonly eaten, they are found on two of the most common and widespread trees in Central Australia and are therefore, when available, quite an important component of the traditional Aboriginal diet.

The larger of the two, the bloodwood apple, is found on various bloodwoods throughout most of Australia. There are many types of smaller galls in Central Australia but only one, the mulga apple found on *Acacia aneura*, is of any importance. Formed by a wasp, it is about the size and shape of a marble. The grubs found in the gall and the gall itself, or a portion of it, are eaten in both cases. There is little doubt that the grub is the most nutritious part of this food source.

Edible gum or sap

Plants often exude gums and saps from their branches and trunks but not all of these are edible. Many of them have a noxious taste, but even those that appear edible can sometimes cause intestinal upsets. Aboriginal people of Central Australia consider the gums as something of a treat and know just which are edible or not. Although these food sources are rarely found in large quantities and are usually dissolved by heavy rain, they are considered to be something of a delicacy and are much sought after, especially by children.

Mushrooms

As far as I am aware the conventional type of mushrooms (gill-fungi) are never eaten. This type of mushroom is only found in any quantities in Central Australia in exceptionally good seasons and it appears that few of them are, in fact, edible. The desert truffle, *Choiromyces aboriginum*, found only under the ground, is an important and delicious food when in season. As a bonus it also provides potable water, but unfortunately this fungus is now rare in Central Australia.

PLANT FOODS — A WARNING

Anyone who has the impression after reading this book that they could easily survive on plant foods in the desert will soon be disappointed. Inexperienced people will find that most of the food plants are not easily located and that many appear unappetising to those of us reared on a diet of sweet and varied flavours. A keen appetite and a great deal of skill are required to make a living in the desert.

It must also be emphasised that a considerable amount of botanical knowledge is required to recognise certain bushtucker (especially the *Solanum* species). As there are many poisonous plants in Central Australia it is essential that readers follow the advice of an expert before sampling most native foods and medicine.

OTHER PLANT USES
Plant medicines

Many Aboriginal people living in Central Australia still use traditional plant remedies, and at least 70 plant species either are or were used for medicinal purposes. Some of the remedies were regularly used by non-Aboriginal settlers until recent times, and the ones I have used appear to be effective.

Most western medicines have certain characteristics in common: they usually have an unpleasant taste and a strong odour and are poisonous if taken in large quantities; they are generally most popular if they have an immediate effect and they must be readily available. It is probably not surprising that most of the traditional medicines also exhibit these characteristics.

Nevertheless there are some obvious differences. Firstly, few of the Aboriginal medicines are taken internally (less than ten per cent) and secondly, few are used for very specific purposes. These differences are probably related to Aboriginal people's traditionally nomadic lifestyle. If one is often on the move it is better to concentrate on a range of plants with a wide spectrum of uses, for the specific plant you need for a particular ailment may be miles away just when you need it. Also, most powerful internal remedies can be poisonous if the active principle is not carefully measured, and the nomadic people had neither accurate measuring devices nor the equipment required for intricate preparation techniques.

The use of fumes from heated leaves as a healing

agent is widespread and it is now often referred to as a smoking process — for example, 'we smoked the babies to make them strong'. With small children this process usually means holding the children in the fumes for a few minutes. With sick adults, however, the process is often more elaborate. A pit a little larger than the person to be treated is dug, and a fire lit within. When the fire has died down to hot coals, branches from the plant are put on the coals and the sick person lies down upon the leaves and coals until the fumes have ceased. The patient is bathed with the fumes, at the same time inhaling them and no doubt sweating profusely as well. This treatment is said often to cure the patient completely.

Some of the medicinal plants used produce a sap or resin which is dabbed onto a wound or other ailment; ashes produced by burning bark and other plant portions are also used, sometimes being first mixed with ochre or fat. Some of the highly aromatic plants are not treated in any way but are used as pillows or placed in the nasal septum. These plants emit strong odours when crushed and inhalation of the vapours is reputed to help cure chest complaints and related ailments.

Water from plants

The first non-Aboriginal people to enter Central Australia were often perplexed by the presence of Aboriginal people in areas which appeared to be waterless. It is true that the local people often used wells which were not seen by the explorers, but in at least some instances it is highly likely that Aboriginal people were obtaining water from plants: either from the roots or other fleshy organs, or from hollows in the trunks of certain trees. Emergency water can be obtained from the leaves of the fleshy *Calandrinia* plants or from the small swollen roots of the lily *Thysanotus* (not listed here). The desert truffle and the bush potato provide considerable moisture and certain plants are recognised as good indicators of underground water. When conditions are suitable, dew is collected from plants, and knowledge of which dry grass is appropriate to act as a type of sponge in this collecting process is important.

In past times it was only in mid-summer, when one needs to drink large quantities of water to stay alive, or during severe droughts that people were forced back to permanent waters. During the cooler months in normal years their superb knowledge of just how and where to obtain every possible source of water enabled them to travel with impunity over all but the most inhospitable areas of this dry continent.

Wood for implements and weapons

Hunters and gatherers are highly dependent on wooden implements and weapons, and these are generally skilfully made and have multiple uses. In the past, fashioning these objects with stone tools was laborious and time consuming; it was important to know exactly which woods were suitable for specific objects and to have a keen appreciation of their working characteristics. To spend days fashioning an implement only to have it split at the final stages would have been disheartening to say the least.

Central Australian Aboriginal people use the wood from at least 33 different plants. Some, such as mulga, are used to produce a wide range of products while others, such as spearwood (*Pandorea*), have limited — albeit specific — application. Because of their need for mobility, hunters and gatherers must make do with few material possessions and so Aboriginal people have always been masters of the art of flexibility and improvisation. If they required a wooden implement for a specific purpose they knew from just which plant it could be obtained with the least effort or, if it was not immediately available, which plants could be used as a substitute.

Cementing and adhesive substances

An extremely important component of Aboriginal technology is the cementing substance obtained from soft spinifex (*Triodia* species) and it is hard to imagine survival in the desert without it. This resinous material is vital for the construction of the *tulas* (the basic woodworking tool) but it is also used in the construction of many other implements or to repair broken ones. Spinifex resin is an extremely versatile and useful substance. Although it loses its strength when heated it can be moulded into any shape and re-used time and time again. For this reason it is one of the most important plant products used by desert Aboriginal people, although collection and preparation of the substance is complicated and time consuming.

Resin-bearing spinifexes do not occur in the southern

areas of Central Australia and in the south-west, desert mulga (*Acacia minyura*) and desert grasstree (*Xanthorrhoea*) provide the crucial resin. In the south-east the roots of *Leschenaultia* plants are used. There are other substitute materials too, but none is as strong and useful as the spinifex resin, and the majority are water soluble, so they have limited application. For these reasons spinifex resin was probably an important trading item in the areas in which it occurs.

Plant fibres

Plant fibres are used for a variety of purposes — for example to make ropes and bark sandals, or to wrap and tie up ceremonial objects and trading items — but they do not play a very important role in the economy of Central Australian Aboriginal people. Generally, they were used only when animal materials were not readily available. String bags and fish nets, which require large amounts of twine, do not appear to have been made in the area and most of the twine used was either spun from human or animal hair, or made from kangaroo and emu sinews.

Plants used as an aid in capturing game

In suitable areas the use of plant poisons to capture emus and other game is a common practice. These plant poisons are applied to small waterholes and the animals drinking from them become stupefied and are easily captured. The plant most often used is *Duboisia hopwoodii* but if it is not available one of at least three other species can be used.

Other plant-centred hunting methods include: capturing small kangaroos by using long brush fences to channel the animals into a concealed pit; using branches to construct hides from which emus can be speared as they come to drink at a waterhole; constructing a type of fish net from spinifex tussocks or the branches of the tea-tree. In addition, the sticky vines of the *Boerhavia* plant are used to entangle the small birds that come to drink at waterholes, and the thorny branches of *Capparis* bushes prove effective in catching bats. The special shape and texture of the stems of *Enteropogon* grass means they can be used as hooks to extract grubs from tree trunks.

Plants and the religious life

Plants, like all natural objects, play an important role in Aboriginal religion, but much information is restricted to those initiated into the Tjukurrpa, the Altyerre or the Wapar — the Dreaming, as it has come to be known.

According to the Tjukurrpa, the Dreamtime ancestors who created all living things are still present and are now represented by natural objects. Most of the natural features of the landscape were formed by their activities and certain of them contain the 'life essence' of various plants and animals. To ensure the continued existence of these plants and animals, ceremonies must be carried out at these sites. These rituals are usually referred to as 'increase ceremonies', but as this term implies a progressive unnatural increase of the particular organisms, the term 'maintenance ceremony' is probably more apt. Maintenance ceremonies are regularly carried out throughout much of Central Australia for most of the plants discussed in this book.

Plant ornaments and decoration

Although ochres and animal materials are usually preferred for decorative purposes, plant material often plays an important role in this aspect of Aboriginal life. About 30 Central Australian plants are used in some way or another for this purpose, especially in relation to ritual objects and ceremonies.

Fire

Fire is an integral part of Aboriginal life, and knowledge of the burning qualities of various plants is essential. Certain grasses are required to get a flame started after the initial part of the fire-making procedure; other plants can be relied upon to burn when wet. On the other hand, twining plants that resist fire are also important as they are used to produce burnt and unburnt patterns on wooden artefacts. The use of slow-burning woods means that less effort is required in stoking the fire during the night and certain other woods produce copious smoke to fend off troublesome insects. The knowledge of which plants burn slowly while providing good illumination is important in the construction of torches.

MAP OF THE AREA COVERED IN THIS BOOK

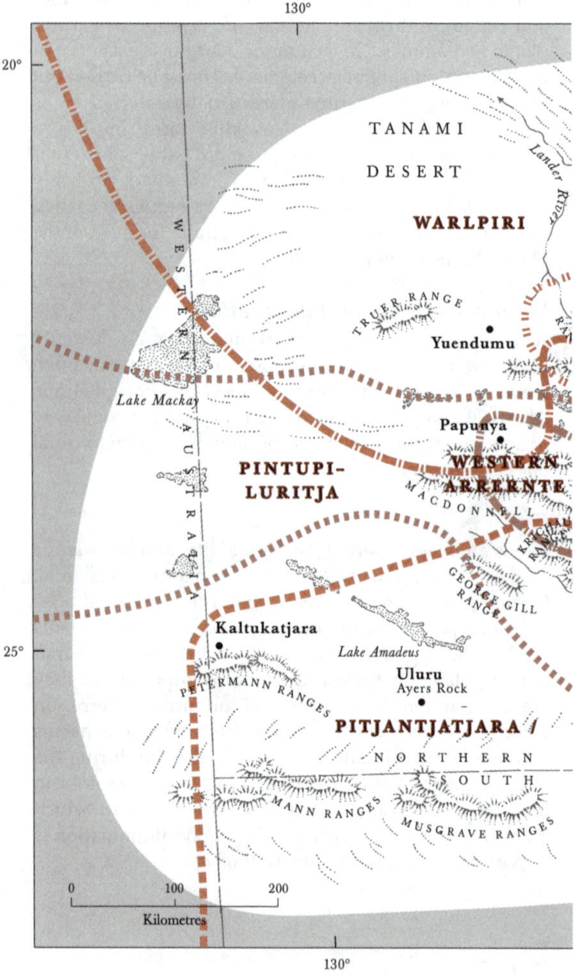

The languages spoken in Central Australia which are represented in this book are Pitjantjatjara, Warlpiri, Pintupi, Arrernte (Eastern and Central), Western Arrernte, Alyawarr, Anmatyerr (Eastern and Western) and Kaytetye (included for the first time in this pocket edition). Their approximate distribution is shown on the map. Yankunytjatjara and Pintupi–Luritja are also shown, but have not been included in the text because of limited space, time and available information.

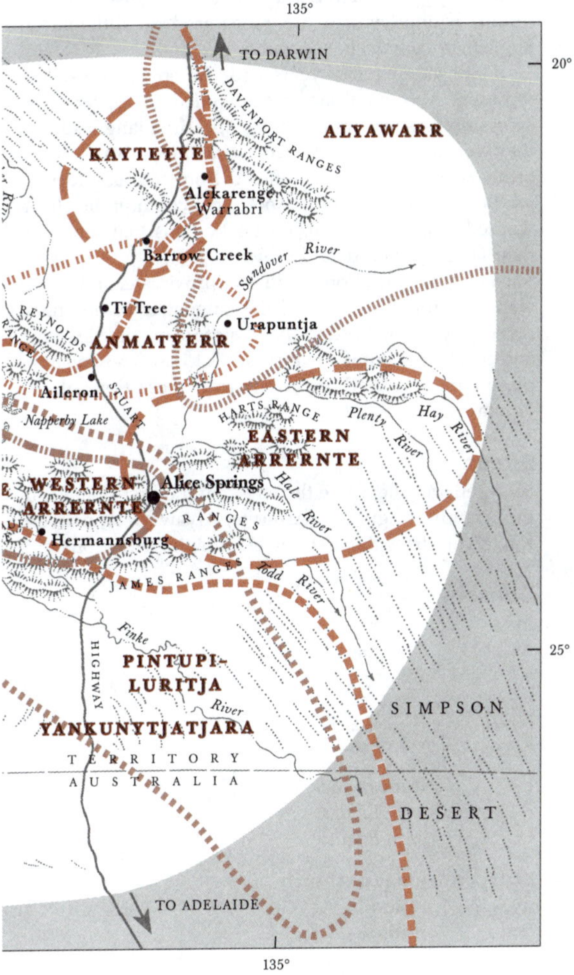

CENTRAL AUSTRALIAN ABORIGINAL LANGUAGES

To the novice, the orthographies or writing systems now used to represent Central Australian Aboriginal languages can be quite opaque, stuffed with a jumble of consonants in unfamiliar combinations. This is because these languages do use a range of sounds which don't occur in English. (They also don't distinguish between certain sounds which are recognised as different in English, notably **p/b**, **t/d** and **k/g**.)

Until about thirty years ago, the spellings used to represent Aboriginal languages tended to appear more accessible to speakers of English as a first language; but they were approximations rather than properly organised orthographies, and they suffered from serious practical problems. Recently many Aboriginal communities have worked with linguists to devise systems that represent their languages more faithfully.

This pronunciation guide is approximate, and if you want to pronounce any of the languages in this book correctly you will need to spend quite some time learning and practising. But if all you want is to say a few plant or place names in Warlpiri or Arrernte, these tips will get you fairly close.

Stress

As a general rule, place the stress on the first syllable. In the Arandic languages (Arrernte, Alyawarr, Anmatyerr, Kaytetye), stress the first vowel following a consonant.

Consonants

m	*as in English*
w	*as in English*
y	**y**acht
p	**b**ad or **p**ad
k	**c**ut or **g**ut
t	**d**uck or **t**uck
n	*as in English*
l	*as in English*
j / ty / tj	ju**dg**e or **ch**urch
ny	o**ni**on
ly	mi**lli**on

th	**th**ere (place tip of tongue between teeth)
nh	**n**o (place tip of tongue between teeth)
lh	**l**ow (place tip of tongue between teeth)
rt / ṯ	po**rt**er (sound the **r**, as with a N. American accent)
rn / ṉ	mo**rn**ing (sound the **r**, as with a N. American accent)
rl / ḻ	whi**rl**ing (sound the **r**, as with a N. American accent)
r	*as in English*
rr	**r**olled, as with a Scots accent
rd	flapped **r** (Warlpiri only)
ng	si**ng**er
ngk	fi**ng**er

Complex consonants

These may need practice, especially when they occur at the beginning of a word.

pm	u**pm**ost
tn	chu**tn**ey
tnh	chu**tn**ey (place tip of tongue behind upper front teeth)
rtn	bi**rd n**est (sound the **r**, as with a N. American accent)
tny	eat**'n y**our dinner (Australian accent)
kng	A**gn**es

Vowels

Arrernte, Alyawarr, Anmatyerr, Kaytetye

a	f**a**ther
e	**a**fter
we	c**oo**k
ey	f**ee**t
i	**ai**r, s**ee** or **i**t
u (initial vowel)	p**u**t
u (after consonant)	m**o**re

*Initial **a** and final **e** are often left out in casual speech*

Pitjantjatjara, Pintupi, Warlpiri

a	f**a**ther
i	h**i**d
u	p**u**t

You may find it interesting to look at these words and place names, and compare the current spellings with older versions, or with the English words from which they are borrowed:

Current spelling	Older spelling /source	Meaning
akngwelye	gnoilya	dog (Arrernte)
Nthareye	Ntaria	Hermannsburg (W. Arrernte)
Alekarenge	Ali Curung	*formerly* Warrabri (Kaytetye)
panipake	*from* 'funny bugger'	amusing person (Arrernte)
mwetekaye	*from* 'motorcar'	car (Kaytetye)
terethe	*from* 'dress'	dress (Kaytetye)
watelwepere	*from* 'white lubra'	white woman (Arrernte)
kalukuwu	*from* 'calico'	tent (Warlpiri)
yungkiyi	*from* 'junk'	rubbish, rubbish tip (Warlpiri)
tjitjamilani	*from* 'teach' (+ verb ending)	(Pitjantjatjara)

GRASSES
and
SEDGES

NATIVE LEMON GRASS, SCENT GRASS, SCENTED OILGRASS
Cymbopogon ambiguus
Family: Poaceae

Alyawarr	*aherr-aherr*
Anmatyerr	*aherr-aherr*
W. Arrernte	*herre-herre*
Kaytetye	*areyneng-areyneng*
Pintupi	*yawula*
Pitjantjatjara	*ilintji*
Warlpiri	*kalpalpi, karrinyarra* (also place name of Mt Wedge), *minjinpa, pajarnpajarnpa, palpalpi, yayirri-yayirri*

Erect, clumped perennial grass to 1 m. **Leaves** bluish-green when young, becoming reddish. Clustered **seed heads** very hairy.

Habitat: Restricted to rocky hillsides, although a form with narrow grey-green leaves also occurs in watercourses or near hills.

Uses: Important medicinal plant throughout the area. Crushed leaves emit a strong scent, inhaled for chest complaints. Leaves and roots are crushed and soaked in water; the liquid is drunk or rubbed on the body for most ills, but especially colds. One of the few Central Australian medicinal plants that is occasionally taken internally.

Ref: *Bushfires & Bushtucker* p. 156

YALKA, ONION GRASS, NALGOO
Cyperus bulbosus
Family: Cyperaceae

Alyawarr	*irreyakwerr*
E. Anmatyerr	*yerrakwerr, irreyakwerr*
W. Anmatyerr	*yerrakwerr*
E. Arrernte	*irreyakwerre, yalke*
W. Arrernte	*yalke*
Kaytetye	*yerrakwerre, erreyakwerre*
Pintupi	*alka, kinyuwurru, tjanmata, yalka*
Pitjantjatjara	*kuraltja, tjanmata*
Warlpiri	*janmarra, kinyuwurru, pinti-parnta, pirlapanu, yakanku, yirrakurru*

Nondescript annual sedge. **Leaves** grassy. **Seed heads** chocolate-brown. **Roots** produce numerous small bulbs up to 10 cm underground. Grows only in warmer months.

Habitat: Mostly in sandy soils close to watercourses and salt lakes.

Uses: One of the most important food plants in Central Australia, especially during dry periods: bulbs are nearly always available. The plant's abundance in favoured habitats means large amounts can be gathered. Women sometimes dig a trench at the edge of a patch then work in a line, turning over the ground, picking out bulbs as they go. Bulbs are sometimes eaten raw, but generally shaken with hot coals in a wooden dish to improve the flavour and facilitate the removal of skins.

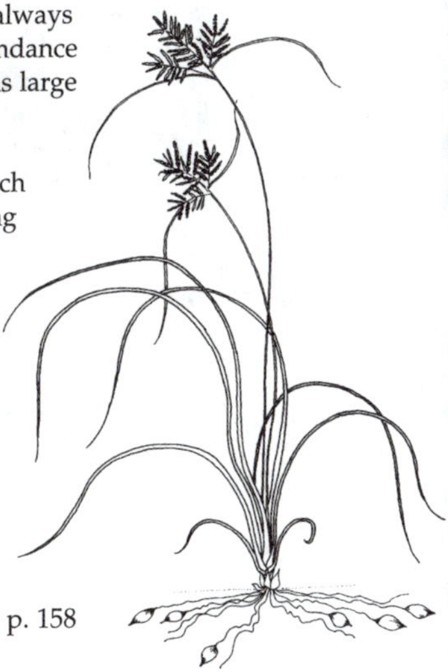

Ref: *Bushfires & Bushtucker* p. 158

BUTTON GRASS
Dactyloctenium radulans
Family: Poaceae

Alyawarr	*apwert-arlkwenh*
E. Anmatyerr	*apwert-arlkwenh, ngelyerr*
E. Arrernte	*ngelyerre*
W. Arrernte	*irntarlkweye, wanyewanye*
Kaytetye	*ngelyerre*
Pintupi	*miyarr-miyarrpa, purruntjari*
Pitjantjatjara	*kanytjil-kanytjilpa*
Warlpiri	*pintaru, puntaru, wirliya pintaru* (= quail track)

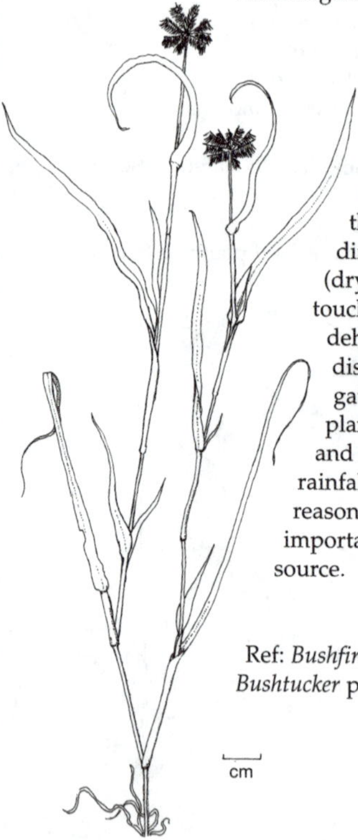

Annual grass: ground hugging, or up to 25 cm high. Quick growing and short lived.

Habitat: Usually in richer soils.

Uses: Seed eaten throughout the area. Usually difficult to gather and clean (dry seed heads fly apart when touched) and tiresome to dehusk, but can be found discarded near ants' nests and gathered more easily. The plant is prolific and can grow and set seed after even small rainfalls, so is probably a reasonably important food source.

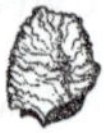

Ref: *Bushfires & Bushtucker* p. 160

CURLY WINDMILL GRASS
Enteropogon acicularis and *E. ramosus*
Family: Poaceae

Alyawarr	*tunper*
E. Arrernte	*tunpere* (?), *twenper*
Kaytetye	*eylwenke* (= hook)
Pitjantjatjara	*ilintji, mukul-mukulpa*

Clumped perennial grasses to 1 m high. **Leaves** usually curl when dry. **Seed heads** windmill-like, about the circumference of a saucer.

Habitat: *E. ramosus:* usually on edges of watercourses; *E. acicularis:* is usually found in shade zones of larger trees.

Uses: Wiry stems make a hook to extract witchetty grubs from trunks of trees. (Grows conveniently at the base of most large trees throughout the area and has long stiff stems and a branching structure which makes a small, strong hook.) Warlpiri people use this plant, probably as a type of sieve, for mixing sugarbag (honeycomb from native bee) with water before eating.

Ref: *Bushfires & Bushtucker* p. 167

E. acicularis

GRASS

WOOLLYBUTT
Eragrostis eriopoda
Family: Poaceae

Alyawarr	*alyatywereng, antyer*
E. Anmatyerr	*alyatywereng*
W. Anmatyerr	*antyey*
E. Arrernte	*antyere*
W. Arrernte	*ntyere*
Kaytetye	*alyatywerenge*
Pintupi	*nantjuri, wangunu*
Pitjantjatjara	*ngutjanu, wangunu*
Warlpiri	*wangunu, warnaralpa, ngurlu* (= edible seed)

Erect, stiff, perennial grass forming dense tufts about 35 cm high. **Leaves** short, rigid, pointed. Dense white woolly **butts** at base of plant (often hidden by stems) are characteristic. **Seeds** small, reddish; produced a month or two after summer rains.

Habitat: All habitats except those with clayey soils. Most common under mulga where it often forms dense stands.

Uses: Seeds are a traditional staple throughout area. Although tiny, large amounts can be collected, cleaned and ground fairly easily. A paste made with water is cooked in hot sand and ashes; cooked loaves can be stored for considerable periods. Nutritionally equivalent to or better than whole wheat. White woolly basal hairs are sometimes used for decoration during ceremonies. Seed paste is sometimes used as medicine (Pit.).

Ref: *Bushfires & Bushtucker* p. 169

LOVE GRASSES
Eragrostis species
Family: Poaceae

Alyawarr	*awertaw*
E. Anmatyerr	*awertaw*
E. Arrernte	*awertawe*
Kaytetye	*awertawe*
Pintupi	*irriya, yirriya*

(Several *Eragrostis* species are utilised but rarely have discrete Aboriginal names.)

E. dielsii: erect or spreading annual or short-lived perennial with cylindrical spikelets, often curved to one side of axis. Occurs throughout area, most commonly in saline or semi-saline areas.

E. falcata: a salt-tolerant variable species very similar to *E. eriopoda*, but without thick woolly butts. Usually found growing with *E. dielsii*.

E. leptocarpa: a delicate annual with fine seed heads, found growing in damp areas.

E. setifolia: similar to the others but only grows in non-saline clayey soils.

Uses: Seeds of all four, and probably several other species, are used in the same way as woollybutt seeds.

Ref: *Bushfires & Bushtucker* p. 168

E. leptocarpa

LUKARRARA, DESERT SEDGE
Fimbristylis oxystachya
Family: Cyperaceae

E. Anmatyerr	*akwetelh*
Kaytetye	*akwetelhe*
Pintupi	*lukarrara*
Warlpiri	*lukarrara*

Erect, annual sedge, about 30 cm. Has few basal **leaves**. Grows quickly after summer rains; most common in first season after a fire.

Habitat: Occurs either on sandplains or lateric rises, with spinifex.

Uses: Seeds, eaten by Pintupi and Warlpiri people, are considered to produce a 'sweet damper' and are a reasonably important food source.

The perennial *F. eremophila* is given the same name by the Warlpiri and its seed is similarly utilised.

Ref: *Bushfires & Bushtucker* p. 198

NATIVE MILLET
Panicum decompositum
Family: Poaceae

GRASS

Alyawarr	*altywart*
Anmatyerr	*altywart*
E. Arrernte	*altyartwe*
W. Arrernte	*altywert*
Kaytetye	*altywarte*
Pintupi	*iltju_t_a, tja_l_kara, ya_l_kara*
Pitjantjatjara	*ka_l_tu-ka_l_tu, tarkau_l_tu*
Warlpiri	*yika, yurlumpuru*

Short-lived perennial grass about 70 cm. **Foliage** bluish-green. **Seed heads** large, diffuse; become detached from plant at maturity and are blown about by wind. Appears after summer rains; seeds usually available in late summer or early autumn.

Habitat: Widespread but most common in somewhat clayey, better-watered soils.

Uses: Seeds are an important food throughout the area: abundant and relatively easy to gather. Thin outer husks are rubbed off between the hands; seeds are ground and cooked to form an unleavened loaf. The hard inner husk is not removed, so the fibre content is higher than that of the major grass seed plant, *Eragrostis eriopoda* (p. 20). The nutritional value is similar.

Ref: *Bushfires & Bushtucker*
p. 240

SPINIFEX, PORCUPINE GRASS
Triodia species
Family: Poaceae

Alyawarr	*aywert*
Anmatyerr	*aywert, irrkwal* (E. Anm.)
Arrernte	*aywerte*
Kaytetye	*aywerte, errkwarle*
Pintupi	*tjanpi*
Pitjantjatjara	*tjanpi, tjanti, pila*
Warlpiri	*janpi, yipiri, manangkarra* (=spinifex plain)

References to spinifex in this text refer only to *Triodia* species, not to plants in the genus *Spinifex* which have a coastal distribution and a very different appearance.

Spinifex is the dominant plant over vast areas of Central Australia, occupying between half and two-thirds of the area covered by this book. Central Australian spinifex falls into two major groups. 'Hard' or 'porcupine' spinifexes are non-resinous and have closely packed, rigid leaves: it is almost impossible to put your hand into a tussock. 'Soft' spinifexes are resinous and have less rigid leaves, fairly loosely arranged: with care, a hand can be placed in the tussock.

Individual species are often difficult to differentiate, and Aboriginal terminology for different species also appears somewhat confused; the Aboriginal names listed here are tentative, and need clarification. (Various terms for specific parts of plants have generally not been included.)

There are 20 or so species in the area; only the most important are listed here. Aboriginal uses of these plants are listed in detail only for *T. pungens* (p. 27). Many would also apply to most of the other species.

Ref: *Bushfires & Bushtucker* p. 288 (as *Triodia* and *Plectrachne* species)

HARD SPINIFEX, PORCUPINE GRASS
***Triodia basedowii* and *Triodia* species**
Family: Poaceae

Alyawarr	*aywert*
E. Anmatyerr	*aywert*
E. Arrernte	*arranke*
Kaytetye	*aywerte*
Pintupi	*untiya, mankalpa* (?)
Pitjantjatjara	*awilura*
Warlpiri	*yintulkanji*

Perennial hummock grass about 40 cm high. At first rounded in shape, but dies out in centre to form rings 2–3 m in diameter. **Leaves** greyish-green, sharply pointed. **Seed heads** hairy, often purplish, borne on stalks about 40 cm long. Flowers after good rains. Other hard spinifexes, except buck spinifex (*T. longiceps*, p. 26) look similar to *T. basedowii* and are generally differentiated only by seed-head characteristics. They are restricted to gravelly hillside slopes.

Habitat: Spinifex sandplains, sandhills and low hills. Occupies about half total area of sandplains and dune fields. Seems to be restricted to areas where there is limestone or gravel 2–4 m or so beneath sand.

Uses: Uses are minor; but plants are important as a vector for fire. See *T. pungens* (p. 27).

Ref: *Bushfires & Bushtucker* p. 289

GRASS

BUCK SPINIFEX, BULL SPINIFEX
Triodia longiceps
Family: Poaceae

Alyawarr	*ntwemerr*
E. Anmatyerr	*ntwemerr, untemerr, arrangk*
Kaytetye	*ntwemerre*
Pitjantjatjara	*tjiri* (?)
Warlpiri	*pujuwaja, janykurlu* (?) (thick dense spinifex in general)

Largest 'hard' spinifex. Forms spiny hummocks up to 1.5 m high and 2 m wide. **Leaves** bluish-green, particularly stiff and sharp.

Habitat: Usually restricted to calcareous soils.

Uses: See *T. pungens*. A particularly obnoxious plant, usually given a wide berth by Aboriginal people.

Ref: *Bushfires & Bushtucker* p. 289

SOFT SPINIFEX
Triodia pungens
Family: Poaceae

Alyawarr	*alatyeyt*
Anmatyerr	*alatyeyt*
E. Arrernte	*alatyite*
W. Arrernte	*walke*
Kaytetye	*alatyeyte*
Pintupi	*tjapuru, tjinalpa*
Pitjantjatjara	*tjapuṟa*
Warlpiri	*marna* (grass), *manyangarnpa, kalajirdi*

Resin

Alyawarr	*anker*
E. Anmatyerr	*anker*
W. Anmatyerr	*tyalangk*
E. Arrernte	*ankere*
W. Arrernte	*tyalangke*
Kaytetye	*atnkere*
Pintupi	*kiṯi, warrtja-warrtja*
Pitjantjatjara	*kiṯi*
Warlpiri	*palya*

Medicine

E. Anmatyerr	*tyerremp*
Arrernte	*tyerrempe*
Kaytetye	*tyerrempe*

Highly viscid hummock grass, variable size: 0.5–2 m high, 1–3 m wide. **Leaves** green, somewhat rigid. **Seed heads** pale yellowish. **Stalks** up to a metre long. Flowers only in warmer months for 2–3 weeks, about a month after rain. Areas dominated by this plant can resemble large wheatfields.

Habitat: Mostly on red sand abutting mulga; also on sand dune crests, near salt lakes and on isolated hills.

Uses: Important plant. Sticky resin covering plant dries to a whitish granular substance. A complicated procedure used to obtain and treat resin provides a black thermoplastic substance considered to make the strongest cementing agent — an essential item of Aboriginal technology. However, some ants use large quantities of resin to cement sand grains into anthills and small sand tunnels which are also attached to spinifex leaves. Aboriginal people sometimes use the melted-down anthills, strengthened with kangaroo dung or plant fibres; although sand in the mixture makes it an inferior cement.

Warlpiri are said to eat spinifex internodes in times of hardship, but consider them a tasteless, stopgap food. Small ant larvae and eggs are obtained from resinous anthills and eaten, often mixed and ground up with grass seeds. Aboriginal people in this area deny any past use of spinifex seeds for food.

All spinifex, especially this species, are extremely flammable; their importance as a vector for fire cannot be over-emphasised.

Minor uses: Whole plants are used for shelters and windbreaks or, in central area, to make a simple fish net. Portions of plants can be used to shore the sides of deep wells, or to wrap objects for storage. Leaf bunches make good torches, and charred remains are sometimes used to draw black designs on bodies or other objects.

Ref: *Bushfires & Bushtucker* p. 290

BULRUSH, CUMBUNGI, CATTAIL
Typha domingensis
Family: Typhaceae

GRASS

W. Arrernte   *ingkwe*
Pitjantjatjara   *apita* (?), *tjintjira, tjuna-tjuna*

Aquatic plant 1.5–2.5 m high. Stiff brownish **spikes** projecting above large, long, grassy **leaves**.

Habitat: Scattered populations throughout area. Restricted to areas of permanent or semi-permanent water, so most often found in the larger ranges.

Uses: Basal parts are eaten (W. Arr. only). This and close relatives are an important food and fibre source elsewhere in Australia and the world. Never very abundant in Central Australia, it is of minor importance.

Ref: *Bushfires & Bushtucker* p. 294

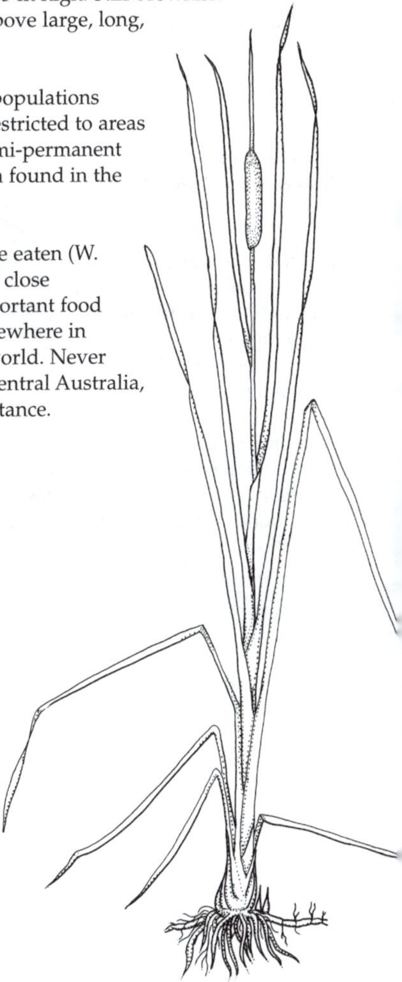

SUMMER GRASS, ARMGRASS MILLET
Urochloa piligera
Family: Poaceae

Alyawarr	*atnyent, atwet*
Anmatyerr	*anekwerr, mamperrk* (?)
W. Arrernte	*itwerte*
Pintupi	*mana*
Pitjantjatjara	*ilirara, kunakanti, kunawitu*
Warlpiri	*yika*

Annual grass. **Stems** weak. **Leaves** broad. **Seed heads** smooth.

Habitat: Throughout area, but less common in south and in sandy spinifex areas; most common on river flats and in other areas with rich sandy soils, usually under trees.

Uses: Important seed plant, especially in central areas. Seeds ripen unevenly and are usually collected from the ground beneath the plant or from ants' nests. Preparation techniques are complicated.

Ref: *Bushfires & Bushtucker* p. 131 (listed as *Brachiaria subquadripara* and *B. piligera*)

RIVER SUMMER GRASS
Urochloa praetervisa
Family: Poaceae

Alyawarr	*awertaw*
Anmatyerr	*awertaw*
Arrernte	*awertawe*
Kaytetye	*awertawe*

Large summer grass, similar to *U. piligera* but larger, with more clustered seed heads. Found throughout the area but needs rich, well-watered soils.

Ref: *Bushfires & Bushtucker* p. 132
(as *Brachiaria*)

DESERT FLINDERS GRASS, BUNCH PANIC
Yakirra australiensis
Family: Poaceae

Alyawarr	*alwepenh, yakerr*
E. Anmatyerr	*alepenh*
W. Anmatyerr	*kwarrety (?), nyetempwer*
Kaytetye	*alepenhe*
Pintupi	*alkara, yalkara*
Pitjantjatjara	*multjalki, putja nyii-nyii* (nyii-nyii = zebra finch), *tjanpi nyii-nyii, tjuti-tjuti*
Warlpiri	*warripinyi, yukarrija, purnujutu*

Dense, rounded annual grass about 15 cm high. **Foliage** often reddish at maturity. **Seed heads** small, mostly hidden amongst foliage. Grows quickly after summer rains. Usually only abundant as pioneer species after fire or drought.

Habitat: Restricted to sandy or gravelly spinifex-dominated areas.

Uses: Seeds are an important food throughout the area, but difficult to collect directly from the plant as they ripen unevenly, fall quickly to the ground and are hidden in sand. However, large amounts are collected: a particular ant species carries seeds back to the nest and chews off part of the seed base, discarding the seed outside the nest. Piles of seeds are gathered easily once the ants' nest is found. Seeds are cleaned, ground with water into a paste and cooked in hot sand and ashes to produce an unleavened loaf. Excess grain is sometimes stored for long periods. High in fibre and nutritional value.

Ref: *Bushfires & Bushtucker* p. 298

HERBS

KEELED LANTERN BUSH
Abutilon otocarpum
Family: Malvaceae

Alyawarr	*akeley-akeley, arlpart, aylpart*
E. Anmatyerr	*aylpat-aylpat, akeley-akeley*
Kaytetye	*akeley-akeleye*
Pintupi	*tatji-tatji*
Pitjantjatjara	*tjirin-tjirinpa*
Warlpiri	*jinka-jinka, taji-taji*

About 50 cm high. **Leaves** broad, covered with dense mat of hair. **Flowers** bright yellow, occurring after rain. **Seeds** curved and wrinkled. Desert lantern (*A. leucopetalum*) is larger, lacks depression at base of fruit and its seeds are not eaten.

Habitat: Widespread; it is often found in shade zones of large trees.

Uses: Only Alyawarr people use the seed of this species: plant is probably not found in large enough numbers to be an important food source except after fires. Seeds are not abundant, but are relatively large and easy to collect, especially as they are often found heaped up beside ants' nests. Seeds have a pleasant nutty flavour and need no preparation.

Ref: *Bushfires & Bushtucker* p. 84

DESERT AMARANTHUS
Amaranthus species
Family: Amaranthaceae

Pitjantjatjara *liru-liru*
Warlpiri *jilkarla-jilkarla*

Erect herbs about 30 cm high. **Flowers** small, rather insignificant and clustered on stem at base of opposite leaves. **Seeds** small, shiny, black.

Habitat: *A. interruptus* is widespread in Central Australia and usually grows on hillsides. It has 'rat-tail' heads due to the absence of upper leaves. *A. grandiflorus* has the largest flowers; it is usually found on sand dunes in the southern third of the area. *A. mitchellii* has the smallest flowers; it is usually found on clayey soils.

Uses: Seeds are sometimes ground and eaten (Warl., Pit.); Alyawarr people soak leaves of *A. mitchellii* to produce a body wash. Otherwise these plants are not much used in Central Australia. Other *Amaranthus* species are cultivated for seed in S. America.

Ref: *Bushfires & Bushtucker* p. 124

Amaranthus mitchellii

TAR VINE
Boerhavia species
Family: Nyctaginaceae

Alyawarr	*ayep*
Anmatyerr	*ayep*
E. Arrernte	*ayepe*
W. Arrernte	*yepe*
Kaytetye	*ayepe*
Pintupi	*wayipa*
Pitjantjatjara	*pilyali, puunpa, wituka, ungka* (roots), *urpa* (growth tips)
Warlpiri	*wayipi*

Creeping herbs; **stems** often trail for up to 1 m. Different species are not well classified but with *B. coccinea* the whole plant is sticky; *B. schomburgkiana* and *B. repleta* are much less sticky. Once established, they put out new growth from rootstock after rain during all but coldest months.

Habitat: Most habitats, but less common in spinifex areas.

Uses: Roots eaten raw or lightly roasted so bitter skin can be easily removed. Flavour is bland and root is fibrous, so of low calorific value; but still an important food source during harsh periods. *B. coccinea* is sticky, and is sometimes spread around small waterholes (Pit.) to trap finches and other small birds.

Ref: *Bushfires & Bushtucker* p. 130

B. diffusa

TAR VINE CATERPILLAR (YEPERENYE OR YIPIRINYA GRUB)

Alyawarr	*arrpayerr*
Anmatyerr	*arrpayerr, ntyarlk, ayepayt*
E. Arrernte	*ayepe-arenye, ntyarlke*
W. Arrernte	*yeperenye*
Kaytetye	*ayepayte*
Pitjantjatjara	*anumara*
Warlpiri	*wayipi-pama*

The caterpillar commonly found on tar vine is also an important food. The larva of one of the large hawkmoths (*Celerio lineata livornicoides*), it is greenish and about five centimetres long. Gathered in large numbers, they are stored for a day or so until ingested plant material has passed through them, then are yandied in wooden dishes to remove dung (or the head is removed and leaf material squeezed out). They are then cooked by adding hot ashes to a coolamon while gently shaking it. Surplus dried insects keep well and can be stored for considerable periods. Yeperenye is an important totemic animal in the Alice Springs area.

PARAKEELYA
Calandrinia balonensis
Family: Portulacaceae

Alyawarr	*alyemp-alyemp, lywemp-lywemp*
Anmatyerr	*arrwelth-arrwelth, lywemp-lywemp, parrkely*
E. Arrernte	*lyempe-lyempe, parrkelye*
W. Arrernte	*ilkngwalye*
Kaytetye	*lywemp-lywempe, parrakelye*
Pintupi	*kumul-kumulpa*
Pitjantjatjara	*nyurngi, parkilypa, tjunngi*
Warlpiri	*parrkilyi, patanjarnngi*

Fleshy herb about 25 cm high. **Leaves** succulent. Attractive pink or purple **flowers**. Germinates after winter rains and lasts longer than most other annuals because of moisture stored in stems and leaves.

Habitat: Usually with spinifex in red sands.

Uses: Seeds, roots and leaves eaten (Pit.). Leaves eaten raw for moisture content only in emergencies. Usually, whole plant is steamed — and then only when more favoured foods are not available. Small black seeds are sometimes gathered, ground to a paste and eaten but they ripen unevenly and much work is needed to obtain useful amounts.

Ref: *Bushfires & Bushtucker* p. 134

SNEEZE WEEDS
Centipeda minima, C. thespidioides
Family: Asteraceae

HERB

Alyawarr	*inteng-inteng*
Pitjantjatjara	*kata-palkalpa*
Warlpiri	*munyu-parnti-parnti*

Variable herb: small, spreading or erect. **Leaves** can be densely hairy to almost glabrous; highly aromatic when crushed. **Flowers** small, greenish, inconspicuous. *C. thespidioides* is similar, with more angular flower heads.

Habitat: Watercourses and swamps. Widespread: rare or absent only in far south-west corner of area. *C. thespidioides* restricted to clayey soils and usually grows in gilgais.

Uses: Aromatic vapours aid in treatment of coughs and colds. Leaves may also substitute for pituri when wild tobacco is not available. Both species are used in the same way, have the same characteristic odour and appear to be given the same Aboriginal names.

Ref: *Bushfires & Bushtucker* p. 145

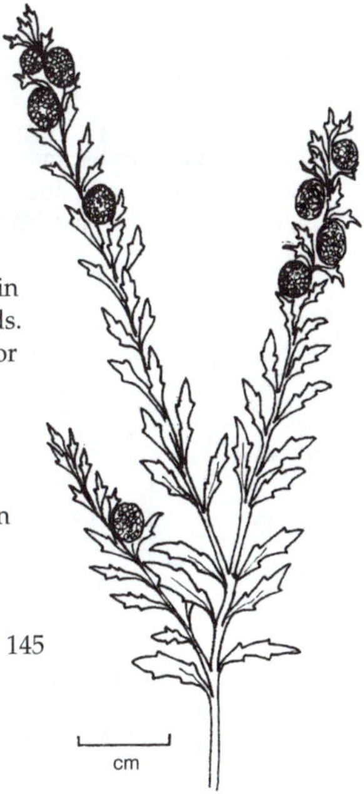

C. minima

TICKWEED
Cleome viscosa
Family: Capparaceae

Alyawarr	*awerr-awerr, irltey-irltey*
E. Anmatyerr	*rltey-rltey*
Kaytetye	*arrematye eyltey-eylteye*
Pitjantjatjara	*ngampul-ngampulpa* (= inedible fruit)
Warlpiri	*kuntinpa*

Sticky herb about 40 cm high. **Flowers** yellow, attractive. **Pods** sub-cylindrical, containing numerous black wrinkled **seeds**.

Habitat: Variety of habitats; often abundant in recently burnt mulga areas.

Uses: Seeds are bitter: may be eaten by Warlpiri people but reports are conflicting — use may be medicinal. Plant has medicinal uses in other parts of Australia and overseas.

Ref: *Bushfires & Bushtucker* p. 148

SANDOVER LILY
Crinum flaccidum
Family: Liliaceae

POISONOUS

HERB

Alyawarr	*ilyelkernng*
E. Anmatyerr	*iylelkennge*
W. Anmatyerr	*lyelkenng, alyelkalyelk*
Kaytetye	*eylelkennge*
Warlpiri	*marnampi, ngarlirl-karlirlki, yarlirl-karlirlki*

Leaves limp, shiny, leathery. **Flowers** white or pink-tinged. **Bulbs** large, onion-like; often found as deep as 0.5 m underground.

Habitat: Watercourses: grassy floodouts and temporary swamps.

Uses: Bulb is either rubbed on sores, boils and itchy areas of skin or a decoction is used as a medicinal wash (E. Warl, N. Anm'rr). In other parts of Australia the bulb is reputedly eaten; in Central Australia it is bitter and considered poisonous.

Ref: *Bushfires & Bushtucker* p. 152

RAT-TAIL GOOSEFOOT, GREEN CRUMBWEED
Dysphania kalpari
Family: Chenopodiaceae

Alyawarr	*alpar*
E. Anmatyerr	*alpar*
W. Anmatyerr	*parntentyarlp*
E. Arrernte	*alpare*
W. Arrernte	*alpare, intweke*
Kaytetye	*kalpare*
Pintupi	*maturra*
Pitjantjatjara	*kalpari*
Warlpiri	*juju-minyi-minyi, karntinpa, munyu-parnta, parntinjarlpa*

Erect, odorous, sticky herb up to 25 cm high. Small clustered **flowers** form 'rat tail' spikes in upper half to two-thirds of plant. **Seeds** small, black, shiny; produced a month after rain and held on plant for some time after. Weed-like species, favoured by fire and other disturbances. *D. rhadinostachya* very similar and has different name (*ngimpalpa*) only in Pitjantjatjara.

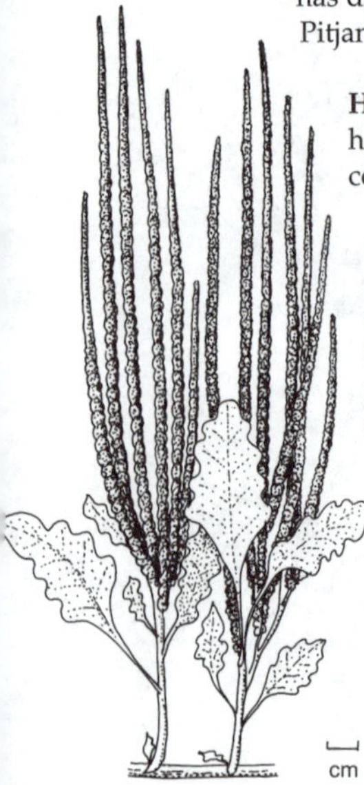

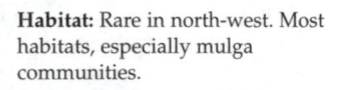

Habitat: Rare in north-west. Most habitats, especially mulga communities.

Uses: Because it is widespread, high in protein and low in fibre, the seed is an important food throughout the area. Seeds are retained on the plant, and are available later in the season than most others. The highly scented leaves are either soaked in water and used as a medicinal wash or ground into powder and mixed with fat for ointment.

Ref: *Bushfires & Bushtucker* p. 164

CAUSTIC WEED, MILK WEED, MAT SPURGE
Euphorbia drummondii
Family: Euphorbiaceae

POISONOUS — **HERB**

Alyawarr	*amwekel-amwekel, aylpaty-aylpaty, mamarlety, manthel, werlaty-werlaty*
E. Anmatyerr	*amwekel, amwekel-amwekel*
W. Anmatyerr	*merterr, amerterr-amerterr*
E. Arrernte	*amerterre, milke-milke, werlatye-werlatye*
W. Arrernte	*ipatye-ipatye, merterre-merterre*
Pintupi	*wunytju-wunytju*
Pitjantjatjara	*ipi-ipi* (plants with milky sap in general), *mangka-mangka*
Warlpiri	*majardi-majardi, malari, pawu-pawu*

Small, ground-hugging herb, usually pinkish. Small, opposite **leaves**. Small **flowers** and small, rounded **fruits** emerge between leaves. Emits milky sap when bruised or broken.

Habitat: Woodland. Widespread, but most common in disturbed areas.

Uses: Warlpiri and Arandic peoples apply sap to skin complaints or use decoction from the whole plant as medicinal wash. In other parts of Australia a decoction is sometimes taken internally. Pitjantjatjara people sometimes place plant on the head, as a type of wig.

Ref: *Bushfires & Bushtucker* p. 195

HEAVY-SOIL HANDFLOWER, TOBACCO HANDFLOWER
Goodenia lunata
Family: Goodeniaceae

Alyawarr	*ankerringk*
E. Anmatyerr	*ankerr-ingka*
W. Anmatyerr	*ntywenart*
E. Arrernte	*arleye-ingke*
Kaytetye	*atarenye*

Herb about 10 cm. **Leaf** shape somewhat variable. **Flowers** yellow, distinctive and usually conspicuous on end of stem.

Habitat: Clay communities throughout area, but less common in south.

Uses: Substitute for pituri (Aly'rr) in absence of favoured *Nicotiana* species (see pp. 48 ff.). Leaves are dried, broken up and mixed with ash before chewing, but considered a poor substitute for the real thing. Sometimes used to poison small waterholes to catch game.

Ref: *Bushfires & Bushtucker* p. 199

DESERT HELIOTROPES
Heliotropium asperrimum and *Heliotropium* species
Family: Boraginaceae

Pitjantjatjara	*mamukaṯa, mamunganpa*
Warlpiri	*jurti-jurti*

Perennial, 30 cm high. **Foliage** bluish-green. Whole plant except flower petals covered in fine irritant hairs. **Leaves** broad with wavy margins. **Flowers** small, white, clustered on one side of flower stalk. **Seed capsules** small and hairy, containing small black seeds.

Habitat: In woodlands, on foothills, or in valleys of ranges formed of crystalline rocks, such as Musgrave and Harts ranges.

Uses: Seeds said to be eaten in times of hardship (Pit.). Separating seeds from capsules is a dreaded chore because of the irritant hairs, but seeds and capsules remain on the plant for long periods and are available even in drought.

Other Heliotropes, especially *H. cunninghamii* (and other short-lived species) are given the same Aboriginal names. *H. cunninghamii* is about 20 cm high with grey-green foliage and small narrow leaves. Hairs are small, fine and less irritant than those of *H. asperrimum*. Occurs throughout the area, generally on lower slopes of spinifex-dominated hills. Seeds reputedly eaten (Pit., Warl.) Decoction of leaves reputedly used as medicinal wash for skin complaints (N. Warl.).

H. cunninghamii

Ref: *Bushfires & Bushtucker* p. 211

ROCK ISOTOME
Isotoma petraea
Family: Campanulaceae

POISONOUS

E. Anmatyerr	*pitherr*
W. Anmatyerr	*anterlp* (?)
W. Arrernte	*irranerratye* (?)
Kaytetye	*ntereympe*
Pintupi	*mara-kanyala*
Pitjantjatjara	*tjuntiwari, wanngati*
Warlpiri	*multu, yarrampa*

Attractive herb or sub-shrub, about 30 cm. **Leaves** soft, green. **Flowers** pale blue.

Habitat: Hills, mostly at base of rocks in sheltered valleys and gorges. Sometimes escapes onto woodland below.

Uses: A very poisonous plant; its juice can cause sore eyes or even temporary blindness. Aboriginal people are well aware of its toxicity; however, they do sometimes mix small amounts of the dried plant with their pituri to increase its potency. Pitjantjatjara people are reputed to use the crushed foliage of this plant as a poultice for the relief of bad headaches.

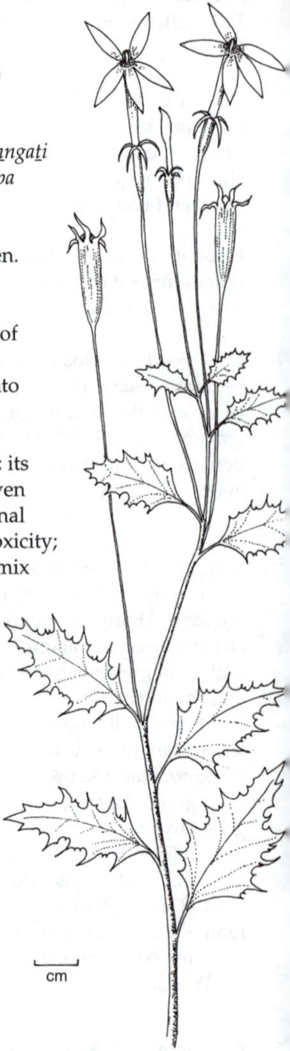

Ref: *Bushfires & Bushtucker* p. 218

MUSTARD GRASS, NATIVE WATERCRESS
Lepidium muelleri-ferdinandi and *Lepidium* species
Family: Brassicaceae

Alyawarr	*irltey-irltey, iyltey-iyltey*
E. Arrernte	*inmartwe*
W. Arrernte	*inmurte*
Pintupi	*inmuṯa*
Pitjantjatjara	*maṉngu-ranytjalpa, unmuṯa*

Erect herb to 20 cm high. **Leaves** narrow. **Flowers** usually insignificant. **Pods** small, oval shaped with small notch at top. *L. oxytrichum* has broader leaves occurring higher up stem; *L. phlebopetalum* has rounded pods and narrow leaves.

Habitat: All three species occur more or less throughout area but are rare in north. Found in non-spinifex areas, growing only after winter rains.

Uses: Aboriginal people apparently utilise the three species in a similar way and do not distinguish between them. Cooked and eaten by all but the Pintupi. (Has a strong flavour similar to watercress when eaten raw.) Plants are uprooted and steamed in a pit, between hot stones or other fleshy plants which modify the sharp taste so that large amounts may be eaten. Leaves and pods are eaten immediately; stems are first hammered to a pulp. Not particularly tasty, but available at a time of year when other foods are scarce.

. *oxytrichum*

Ref: *Bushfires & Bushtucker* p. 219

PITURI, WILD TOBACCO
Nicotiana species
Family: Solanaceae

Alyawarr	*ngkwerlp*
Anmatyerr	*ngkwerlp, arwernp* (W. Anm.)
E. Arrernte	*ingkwelpe*
W. Arrernte	*ngkwerlpe*
Kaytetye	*tyanywenge*
Pintupi	*mingkulpa, ngunu-ngunu*
Pitjantjatjara	*mingkulpa*
Warlpiri	*janyungu, mingkurlpa, ngunju*

In most parts of the world people have been able to derive from plant material a drug that acts upon their central nervous system. Aboriginal people in Central Australia have used pituri. It is a mild drug — about as potent as chewing tobacco — but the four major species used to produce it (all, like the commercial tobacco plant, in the genus *Nicotiana*) are among the most sought after of all Central Australian plants. Chewing pituri is said to reduce thirst and hunger and to produce a general feeling of well-being. It is used by most adults; if *Nicotiana* plants are not available, substitute plants are used.

There is a distinct preference rating of the four species, varying from area to area depending on the concentration of the active principles in the different plant populations. The nicotine content of the various species appears to correspond quite well with the way they are rated. However, nor-nicotine is also found in some species and may play a negative role in the preferent rating of the different pituris, as may the effect of the particular ashes mixed with the quid. Although many people still prefer the native product, commercial tobacco is often used as a substitute and this tends to reinforce the idea that the active constituent is principally nicotine.

Generally the dried plant is broken up and mixed with ash, and rolled into a ball which is held between the lips for a short period then stored behind the ear or in a headband. The ash appears to promote the rapid absorption of the nicotine into the bloodstream through the thin tissues of the lips and mouth, and probably even through the skin behind the ear. At least twelve species of plant are specifically used to produce this ash — not just any ash will do, and it must be free of coals and other unburnt material. All the plant materials used have in common an ability to burn cleanly and produce uncontaminated ash.

All plants of this genus occurring naturally in Central Australia are similar: soft **leaves**, characteristic creamy white, trumpet-shaped **flowers** and smooth, two-valved **seed capsules**. Classification of individual species is difficult and mistakes have often been made. Although Aboriginal people generally recognise the different species, distinct names are not always given and some of the names listed may not be correct. Aboriginal names listed above are generic terms more or less equivalent to the English word 'tobacco'. Other generic terms with wider or more specific meanings for various parts of *Nicotiana* plants and its products are not recorded here.

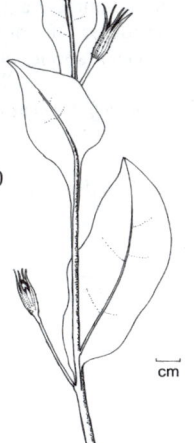

Ref: *Bushfires & Bushtucker* pp. 62, 230

ROUND-LEAVED NATIVE TOBACCO
Nicotiana benthamiana
Family: Solanaceae

Alyawarr	*ngkwerlp-pweter*
Pintupi	*pinapitilypa, tjiknga*
Pitjantjatjara	*tjuntiwari*
Warlpiri	*munju, pirnki-warnu* (= cave-from), *turlkamula* (?)

Soft herb, about 50 cm. **Flowers** creamy, white. Lower **leaves** rounded, with distinct stalks. Germination most frequent in cooler months, especially after fire, but established plants will grow whenever moisture is available.

Habitat: Found in caves and other sheltered areas in hills. Absent from Musgrave and Macdonnell ranges, but occurs on most other smaller ranges and hills throughout area.

Uses: Used as chewing tobacco throughout its range, but considered inferior if other 'stronger' species are available.

See p. 48 ff. for more about pituri.

Ref: *Bushfires & Bushtucker* p. 231

cm

SHINY-LEAVED NATIVE TOBACCO
Nicotiana excelsior
Family: Solanaceae

Anmatyerr	*atnwengk* (?)
E. Arrernte	*pitwerre*
W. Arrernte	*pitwerre*
Pintupi	*wanngati* (?), *warrngati*
Pitjantjatjara	*pulyantu, ukiri, wanngati*

Fleshy herb, about 50 cm. **Leaves** smooth, shiny, clasping stem. Large **flowers**.

Habitat: Hills. Widespread in Musgrave Ranges and also found in calcareous areas in or near Macdonnell Ranges.

Uses: An important plant for Pitjantjatjara people. They know where to find the best stands (usually in caves) and will travel a long way to get them. Plants are dried, in the sun or over a fire, then broken up and made into a quid. Pitjantjatjara consider this species at least as potent as *N. gossei* (p. 52), but Arrernte people generally find *N. excelsior* in their area to be inferior. The chewing quid can be used as cure for ringworm (Pit.). It also plays a part in a rain-making ritual.

See p. 48 ff. for more about pituri.

Ref: *Bushfires & Bushtucker* p. 232

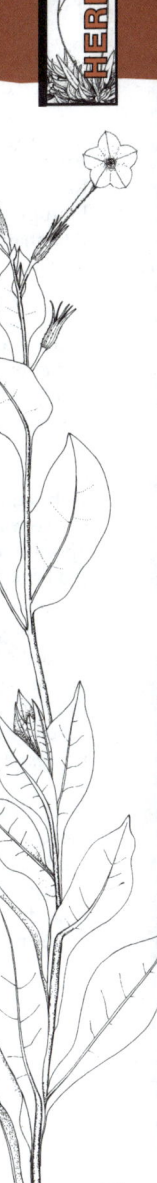

ROCK PITURI
Nicotiana gossei
Family: Solanaceae

Alyawarr	*ngkwerlp rnpernp*
Anmatyerr	*rnpwernp, ngkwerlp urnpernp*
Kaytetye	*tyanywenge rnpernpe*
Pintupi	*tjunpunpa*
Pitjantjatjara	*piturpa*
Warlpiri	*jurnpurnpa, jurnpurnpu*

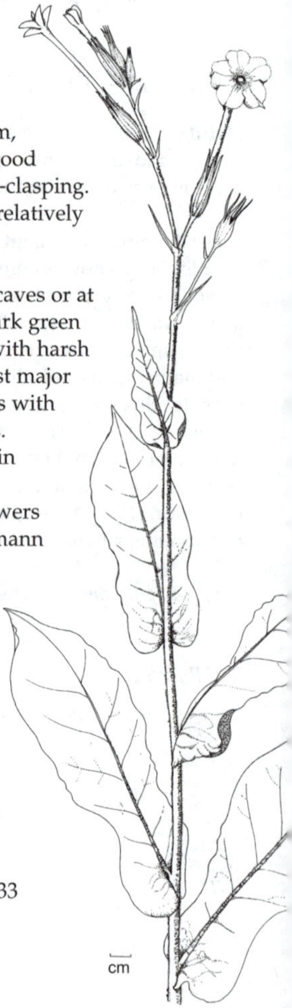

Attractive soft herb about 60 cm, sometimes growing to 3 m in good conditions. **Leaves** fleshy, stem-clasping. White or purplish **flowers** are relatively large.

Habitat: Hills. Often found in caves or at base of rocks where its lush, dark green appearance contrasts sharply with harsh red background. Occurs in most major ranges, but is restricted to areas with most moisture and richest soils. Biggest and best stands found in George Gill Ranges. A slightly different form with smaller flowers occurs in Musgrave and Petermann ranges.

Uses: Probably the single most important plant to Central Australian Aborigines. It is generally regarded as the best pituri and is much sought after.

See p. 48 ff. for more about pituri.

Ref: *Bushfires & Bushtucker* p. 233

SANDHILL PITURI
Nicotiana rosulata ssp. *ingulba*
Family: Solanaceae

Alyawarr	*ngkwerlp atherrk*
E. Anmatyerr	*ngkwerlp atherrk*
W. Anmatyerr	*arwernp*
E. Arrernte	*atnengkwe, pitwerre*
Kaytetye	*tyanywenge atherrke*
Pintupi	*manakarrata, tjurratja*
Pitjantjatjara	*anultja, talyunganu, tawal-tawalpa*
Warlpiri	*yarunpa*

Fleshy herb about 45 cm. **Leaves** smooth, shiny, mostly clustered at base. **Flowers** long, slender, white.

Habitat: Grows in red sands with spinifex or mulga throughout the area, especially after fire.

Uses: Widely available, and plentiful in good seasons, this is the plant most often used for pituri. Potency varies from area to area, but it is generally considered less potent than hill species. Especially important for Pintupi, who do not have more potent species in their country. Juice from the leaves is used to relieve itchy rash caused by contact with processionary caterpillar (itchy grub) (Anm.). Sometimes used to poison small waterholes to catch game (Aly'rr).

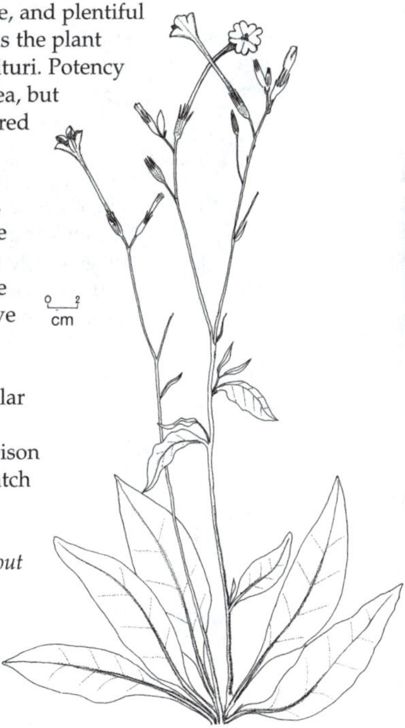

See p. 48 ff. for more about pituri.

Ref: *Bushfires & Bushtucker* p. 235

RUBBISH PITURI
Nicotiana velutina and *Nicotiana* species
Family: Solanaceae

Alyawarr	*kngwarrey-kngwarrey*
Anmatyerr	*ngwarray-ngwarray*
E. Arrernte	*ingkwelpe-ingkwelpe, ingkwerlpe-ingkwerlpe*
W. Arrernte	*ingkwerlp-ingkwerlpe*
Kaytetye	*kngwarraye-kngwarraye*
Pitjantjatjara	*pina-pina, pinar-pinarpa*
Warlpiri	*jungarrayi-jungarrayi*

Soft herb, about 40 cm. **Flowers** short, creamy white or purplish. Highly toxic to stock. A weedy plant, flourishing in disturbed areas.

Habitat: Most habitats but especially abundant on limestone, river banks, or above salt lakes.

Uses: The most often encountered of all the native tobaccos in Central Australia; rarely if ever used by Aboriginal people. *Nicotiana megalosiphon, N. occidentalis* and *N. simulans* also occur in the area, are generally given the same name as this species and are treated with the same indifference.

See p. 48 ff. for more about pituri.

Ref: *Bushfires & Bushtucker* p. 236

N. velutina

MUNYEROO, PIGWEED, PURSLANE
Portulaca oleracea
Family: Portulacaceae

Alyawarr	*lyaw*
E. Anmatyerr	*iylaw*
W. Anmatyerr	*akat*
E. Arrernte	*alyawe, lyawe*
W. Arrernte	*lyawe*
Kaytetye	*eylawe*
Pintupi	*wakati, wayali*
Pitjantjatjara	*maru-maru* (black), *tuntunparara, wakati*
Warlpiri	*patilpinpa, wakati, wayarli*

Fleshy ground-hugging herb, sometimes a metre in diameter. **Flowers** yellow, small, rarely seen. At maturity leaves are shed and pinkish **stems** are exposed. Considered in the past to be co-specific with the world-wide garden weed; now viewed as a separate species. Grows after summer rains and is much favoured by fire.

Habitat: Most abundant in disturbed areas where soils are good, e.g. on watercourse levees.

Uses: Traditional staple food plant throughout the area. Small black seeds, produced in copious numbers, are a most important food. Roots are also cooked and eaten; leaves and stems are used as emergency food, usually only after being steamed. One of the few major food plants which manages to grow and set seed during periods of low rainfall, it has considerable value as an antiscorbutic at these times. Cleaned seeds are ground into an edible paste, either before or after being cooked. Not a particularly delicious food but very nutritious, having high protein and fat levels.

Ref: *Bushfires & Bushtucker* p. 249

APPLE BUSH
Pterocaulon serrulatum
Family: Asteraceae

Alyawarr	*inteng-inteng*
E. Anmatyerr	*inteng-inteng*
E. Arrernte	*pintye-pintye*
W. Arrernte	*pintye-pintye*
Kaytetye	*eynteng-eyntenge*
Warlpiri	*jungarrayi-jungarrayi, munyarni, yanyangi*

Soft, sticky, erect herb about 60 cm high. Often densely hairy, especially on new growth. **Flowers** rather insignificant, clustered; purplish when mature. Crushed **leaves** emit strong, pleasant, apple-like scent. Strongly encouraged by fire.

Habitat: In south, restricted to hillsides; extends onto plains further north.

Uses: Favoured medicinal plant, especially for treating colds. Leaves are either inserted in the nasal septum, used as a pillow, or mixed with fat and used as a rubbing ointment. Considered to have the same properties as Vicks vapour rub. Sometimes used as a tobacco substitute in the north-west of Australia.

P. sphacelatum

Pitjantjatjara	*intiyanu*
Warlpiri	*juju-minyi-minyi, nyinta-nyinta*

Similar, but with smaller leaves and flowers and weaker smell. Usually grows on woodland fringes. Used as above and often given the same name, but not considered as potent.

Ref: *Bushfires & Bushtucker* p. 253

PUSSYTAILS, MULLA-MULLA
***Ptilotus* species**
Family: Amaranthaceae

E. Anmatyerr	*urreyek-alyey-alyey*
E. Arrernte	*awerreke-alyeye-alyeye*, *urreyeke-alyeye-alyeye*
Kaytetye	*awerreke-alyeye-alyeye*
Pintupi	*alputati, yalputati*
Pitjantjatjara	*alputati, liru-liru*
Warlpiri	*jinjirla*

About 18 species (and many varieties) of these attractive plants occur in the area; about ten are widespread. It seems that Aboriginal terminology can vary considerably between and within languages (further investigation is required). Several of the more important plants have, however, been differentiated. See other *Ptilotus* species under sub-shrubs.

LAMB'S TAIL
Ptilotus exaltatus

E. Anmatyerr	*urreyek-alyey-alyey*
E. Arrernte	*awerreke-alyeye-alyeye*, *urreyeke-alyeye-alyeye*
W. Arrernte	*werrekalyeyalyeye*
Kaytetye	*awerreke-alyeye-alyeye*
Pintupi	*ula-ula*
Pitjantjatjara	*alputati, ulawulu*

Annual or short-lived perennial about 60 cm. **Leaves** broad, smooth, glossy, green. **Flowers** pink, strikingly attractive.

Habitat: Gravelly hill slopes.

Uses: The Arandic peoples associate this plant with boys: girls have fun teasing boys by pulling 'their' plant to pieces. Boys, of course, reciprocate.

Ref: *Bushfires & Bushtucker* p. 255

SAND SUNRAY, TIETKINS DAISY
Rhodanthe tietkensii
Family: Asteraceae

Alyawarr	*anteth* (flowers in general)
E. Arrernte	*antethe* (flowers in general)
Pintupi	*wamulu, arrpungu, utalypa, yutalypa, yutal-yutalpa*
Pitjantjatjara	*inma* (= ceremony), *tjulpun-tjulpunpa* (wild flowers in general)
Warlpiri	*tarijirri, wulpayi-wulpayi, wurnpayi-wurnpayi, yunpayi-yunpayi, mardukuru, wamulu* (=fluff, down), *wanjarri* (fluff mixed with red ochre)

Hairy grey-green herb, about 25 cm. **Flowers** yellow.

Habitat: Rare only in far north. Often common in sandy soils after winter rain, especially after a disturbance such as fire or overgrazing.

Uses: One of several plants used to provide down for ceremonial purposes when much-preferred bird feathers are not available in sufficient quantity. When plants are dead and dry, the leaves and flowers can be rubbed off the stem to produce a soft whitish substance. Other species in family Asteraceae also sometimes used for down, and often given the same Aboriginal names, are billy button (*Calocephalus platycephalus*), *Chrysocephalum apiculatum*, *Gnaphalium luteo-album*, *Chrysocephalum semicalvum* and *Myriocephalus stuartii;* also *Gomphrena* species.

Ref: *Bushfires & Bushtucker* p. 212 (as *Helipterum tietkensii*)

BUCKBUSH, ROLYPOLY, TUMBLEWEED
Salsola kali
Family: Chenopodiaceae

Alyawarr	*inkwert*
Anmatyerr	*arlkerl, arlkerlayt* (grub)
E. Arrernte	*arlkerle*
W. Arrernte	*ilkerle*
Kaytetye	*eyleke*
Pintupi	*tjilkala, tjilka-tjilka*
Pitjantjatjara	*tjilkala*
Warlpiri	*jilkarla* (thorn or prickle in general), *putunari, putunarri*

Prickly, rounded annual about 1 m high. **Flowers** and **fruits** inconspicuous. Plant turns yellow at maturity, detaches from its roots and is blown around in wind.

Habitat: Occurs throughout area (and in most other deserts around the world). Usually found in sandy soils.

Uses: A small, white cossid grub found in the thicker portion of the root is eaten throughout area. The biggest and best grubs are usually collected once the plant turns yellow. Grub is readily available over wide areas at certain times of the year, but is small and has a bitter aftertaste, so is probably not an important food source. Mostly gathered only by children.

Ref: *Bushfires & Bushtucker* p. 258

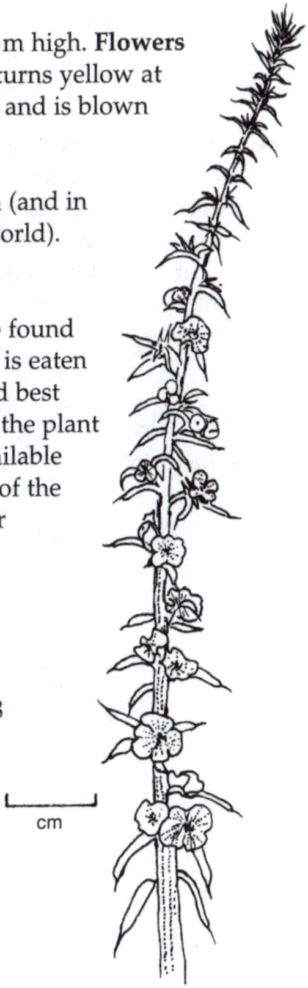

LIFE-SAVER BURR, TEDDY BEAR'S ARSEHOLE
Sida platycalyx
Family: Malvaceae

Alyawarr	*akeley-akeley*
E. Anmatyerr	*akeley-akeley, ingka-mwerney*
E. Arrernte	*awenheye-awenheye*
Kaytetye	*akeley-akeleye*
Pitjantjatjara	*alpuṯaṯi*
Warlpiri	*ngamirdamirdi, pimirdi-pimirdi*

Soft herb or sub-shrub. **Flowers** large, yellow. **Fruit** characteristic, like a prickly doughnut about the size of a twenty-cent piece.

Habitat: Throughout area in most habitats.

Uses: Pitjantjatjara people are said to eat the 'fruit', however it is difficult to imagine a less edible fruit. Possibly the seeds are eaten, but even this is doubtful as they are extremely hard to extract. Warlpiri thread the fruit onto a stick to make a hairbrush. The plant is connected with Alyawarr ceremonies.

Ref: *Bushfires & Bushtucker* p. 267

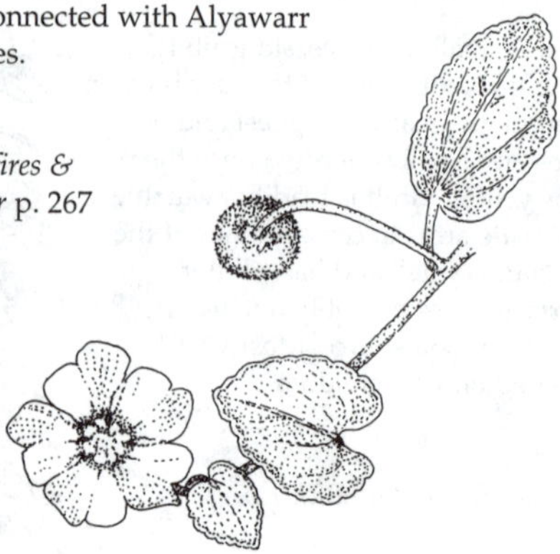

PINTYE-PINTYE, SWEET PILLOW
Stemodia viscosa
Family: Scrophulariaceae

Alyawarr	*inteng-inteng*
E. Anmatyerr	*inteng-inteng*
E. Arrernte	*pintye-pintye*
W. Arrernte	*pintye-pintye*
Kaytetye	*eynteng-eyntenge*
Pitjantjatjara	*intiyanu*
Warlpiri	*manyani, parntinjarlpa*

Erect sticky herb, 25–50 cm. **Flowers** purple. **Leaves** variably shaped. Highly odorous.

Habitat: Moist situations in major range systems.

Uses: Used for medicinal purposes throughout its range, mainly for colds and other chest complaints. May be placed in the nasal septum, used as a cushion to promote restful sleep, or either bruised on a stone or warmed in the fire and placed on the chest. Sometimes a decoction is used as an external wash to cure various internal pains. Also used to strain leaves and other debris from drinking water.

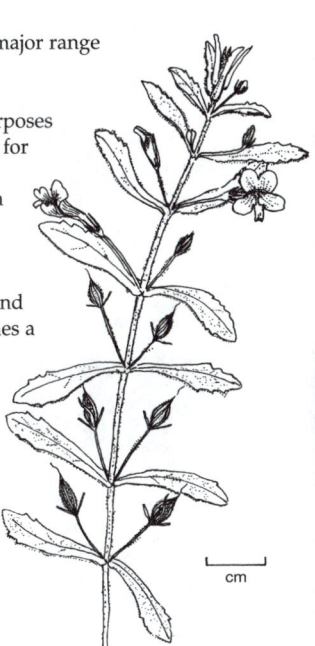

Ref: *Bushfires & Bushtucker* p. 281

SUB-SHRUBS

SANDHILL RATTLEPOD, BIRD FLOWER, DWARF BIRD FLOWER, PARROT PLANT, STUART'S PEA

Crotalaria cunninghamii
Family: Fabaceae

Pintupi	ngalyipi, ngarrtjapiri (?), palykanypa, taliwanti (?)
Pitjantjatjara	ngalyipi, malukuṟu (= kangaroo eye), maḻukuṟu-kuṟu, pinar-pinarpa, taliwanta
Warlpiri	punpunpa

Erect, weak-stemmed shrub to 2.5 m high. **Leaves** soft, grey, velvety. Pea **flowers** large, greenish yellow. **Pods** large, roughly rectangular. Mature pods produce a rattling sound when shaken.

Habitat: Spinifex sandplains and sandhills; usually on bare crests of sand dunes if wild camels have not eaten it away.

Uses: Strong, fibrous bark is used by Pintupi people for sandals (*palykanpa* in Pint., Pit.), to weave into rope used to carry heavy loads and as a lashing in the construction of spears. Elsewhere on the continent decoctions of the leaves are used as eyewash and decoctions of the bark are used to reduce swelling.

Ref: *Bushfires & Bushtucker* p. 153

RUBY SALTBUSH
Enchylaena tomentosa
Family: Chenopodiaceae

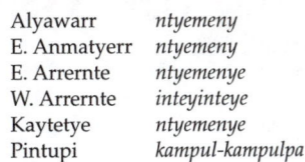

SUB-SHRUB

Alyawarr	ntyemeny
E. Anmatyerr	ntyemeny
E. Arrernte	ntyemenye
W. Arrernte	inteyinteye
Kaytetye	ntyemenye
Pintupi	kampul-kampulpa
Pitjantjatjara	iwatiwata, malkakutjalpa, wilpan-wilpanpa
Warlpiri	mukul-mukulpa

Soft, greyish shrub about 70 cm. **Leaves** cylindrical, succulent. **Flowers** tiny. **Fruits** bright red or yellow and conspicuous. Fruit produced soon after rain.

Habitat: Every habitat; almost always found growing under trees.

Uses: Berries are eaten when ripe and juicy; dried berries are sometimes reconstituted in water, but this is a minor food often eaten only by children. Berries are sometimes used to produce a red dye. They were considered an important antiscorbutic by early European explorers.

Ref: *Bushfires & Bushtucker* p. 166

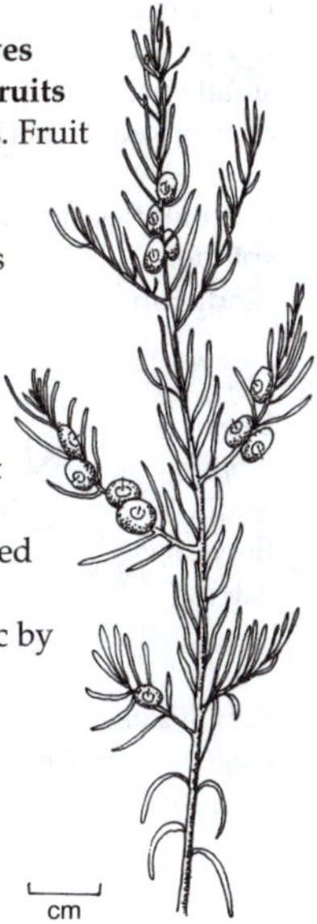

UPSIDE-DOWN PLANT
Leptosema chambersii
Family: Fabaceae

SUB-SHRUB

Alyawarr	*irrarnt-irrarnt*
E. Anmatyerr	*irrarnt-irrarnt*
E. Arrernte	*umpe*
Kaytetye	*errant-errante*
Pitjantjatjara	*ikulyukulyu*
Warlpiri	*patanjarnngi*

Peculiar grass-like plant about 35 cm high. **Stems** stiff, upright, leafless. Large red pea **flowers** hidden away in small clusters at very base of plant and often overlooked. Generally flowers in cooler months of year.

Habitat: Restricted to spinifex sandplains.

Uses: Honey found in the flowers is eaten.

Ref: *Bushfires & Bushtucker* p. 220

WIRE BUSH, TANGLED LESCHENAULTIA
Leschenaultia divaricata
Family: Goodeniaceae

Alyawarr	*anpay, apweneng*
E. Anmatyerr	*unpay*
E. Arrernte	*unpaye*
W. Arrernte	*unpaye*
Kaytetye	*anelyepwete*

Rounded, leafless, clonal sub-shrub about 50 cm. **Stems** tangled, branching. **Flowers** small, yellow. **Seed capsule** sub-cylindrical, about 3 cm long.

Habitat: Eastern half of area, most abundant in south. Usually found close to watercourses in sandy or clayey areas.

Uses: S. Arrernte people obtain a cementing agent from the roots of this plant by heating them and rubbing them onto a stick, producing a plastic substance which hardens on cooling. Apparently it is used as a substitute for resinous spinifex plants (*Triodia* species, p. 24 ff.) which provide the strongest cementing agent but do not occur in the far south-east of the area. Tubers from young plants are eaten (E. Pit., E. Arr. and Aly'rr).

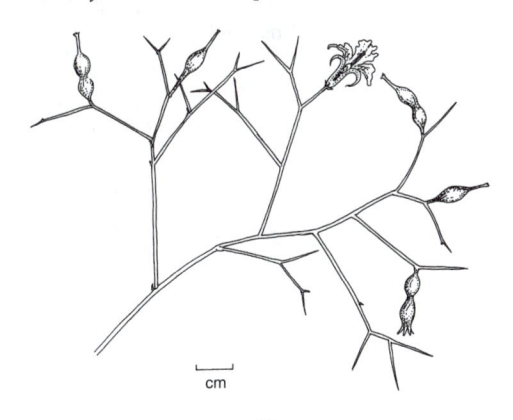

Ref: *Bushfires & Bushtucker* p. 221

SALT DAISYBUSH
Pluchea ferdinandi-muelleri **and**
P. dunlopii
Family: Asteraceae

| Alyawarr | *inteng-inteng, iyter* |
| Warlpiri | *manyani* |

About 70 cm high. **Foliage** either soft greyish-green (*P. ferdinandi-muelleri*), or green and sticky (*P. dunlopii*). **Flowers** pinkish.

Habitat: Watercourses and salt lakes. Can be abundant where spinifex abuts other communities.

Uses: Decoction of the leaves is used as a medicinal wash (Warl., Aly'rr). Related species are used medicinally in other parts of the world.

Ref: *Bushfires & Bushtucker* p. 248 (as *P. tetranthera*)

P. dunlopii

cm

SMOKE BUSH
Ptilotus obovatus
Family: Amaranthaceae

SUB-SHRUB

Alyawarr	*ahert-ahert, irrweny-irrweny, rlkwetherlkwerrng* (?)
E. Anmatyerr	*rlkwetherlkweng, ahert-ahert*
E. Arrernte	*awerreke-alyeye-alyeye* (?)
W. Arrernte	*werre-werre*
Kaytetye	*ahert-aherte, rllkwethelkwerrnge*
Pitjantjatjara	*ku̱ntultji, pu̱rar-pu̱rarpa*
Warlpiri	*mardukuru* (= fluff, down), *warnaparnapa*

Soft, rounded plant about 60 cm. **Leaves** broad, greyish green. **Flowers** rounded, white and pink, rather small. (*P. sessilifolius* is very similar but has somewhat larger flowers and is more or less restricted to woodland communities. Not differentiated by Aboriginal people, and used in same way.)

Habitat: Wide variety of habitats; often grows under trees.

Uses: Edible grubs are found in the roots. Flowers are sometimes used to produce down for ceremonies or for decoration. Soft branches are used to line wooden dishes used for carrying children.

Ref: *Bushfires & Bushtucker* p. 256

SUB-SHRUB

DESERT RAISIN
Solanum centrale
Family: Solanaceae

Alyawarr	*akatyerr*
Anmatyerr	*akatyerr, katyerr*
E. Arrernte	*akatyerre*
W. Arrernte	*katyerre*
Kaytetye	*arlkerre*
Pintupi	*kampurarrpa, kanytjilyi, katarapalpa, kintinyka*
Pitjantjatjara	*kampurarpa, kati-kati*
Warlpiri	*yakajirri, jungkunypa* (ripe fruit), *kampurarrpa, kararrpa, karturu, mulyu*

Clonal under-shrub about 30 cm. **Flowers** purple. **Leaves** rather soft, usually with rusty colouration when young. **Fruit** sticky, yellow when ripe, drying quickly to chocolate-brown colour with raisin-like texture. Fruits produced whenever moisture conditions are suitable but heavy frost can severely reduce crop. Heavily dependent on fire (or other severe disturbances) to obtain maximum potential; absence of fire quickly results in its reduction.

Habitat: Restricted to spinifex sandplains and dune fields and adjacent mulga areas.

Uses: Fruit is probably the most important Central Australian plant food. Widespread and often abundant, the fruit is nutritious and obtainable in some form for most of the year. Dry fruit hangs on the plant for long periods — not very palatable when old and black, but still very nutritious — and can be ground into a paste to eat or rolled into balls to be dried and stored. The Warlpiri are said to distinguish two forms of the plant: *yakajirri*, usually found in mulga country, has a bitter taste; *kampurarrpa*, usually found on sandplains and dune fields, is 'sweet'.

Ref: *Bushfires & Bushtucker* p. 269

BUSH TOMATO
Solanum chippendalei
Family: Solanaceae

SUB-SHRUB

Alyawarr	*anaweyt, anemangkerr, kanakety*
Anmatyerr	hill form: *anakety, antyewarl* (E. Anm.)
	sandhill form: *unemangkerr*
W. Arrernte	*kwere*
Kaytetye	hill form: *kanaketye, antyewarle*
	sandhill form: *kwenemangkerre*
Pintupi	*ngaru, pintalypa, pura*
Pitjantjatjara	*ngaru, pintalypa, pura, wirkalpa*
Warlpiri	*nganjawarli, ngayaki, wanakiji, kakaja, ngaru, kurla-parnta*

Soft clonal shrub usually about 80 cm; up to 1.5 m. **Leaves** grey-green. **Flowers** pale purple. **Fruits** usually globular; change from green or purplish green to pale yellow when ripe. Fruits generally produced whenever moisture conditions suitable, but rarely available during last three months of year. This is a variable species with several forms recognised.

Habitat: Grows with spinifex on sandplains or hill slopes.

Uses: Fruit is a very important plant food throughout its range. The plant is abundant in certain habitats, especially after fire; large amounts of fruit can be quickly and easily gathered. The seeds and thin inner portion are inedible; only the thick outer rind is eaten, and has a bland taste with a slight rockmelon flavour. It is high in vitamin C but has low protein and fat values. Fruit keeps exceptionally well; excess fruits are often threaded onto sticks, dried and stored. Nearly ripe fruit are sometimes lightly roasted to render them edible.

Ref: *Bushfires & Bushtucker* p. 271

BUSH TOMATO
S. diversiflorum

| Pintupi | kakarr<u>t</u>a, ku<u>l</u>a-pa<u>nt</u>a |
| Warlpiri | jarlparrpa, kumpupaja (?) |

Often confused with *S. chippendalei*, (and used in the same way), but has deeply lobed leaves. Grows only in far north-west, but is an important food plant in its restricted area.

Ref: *Bushfires & Bushtucker* p. 275

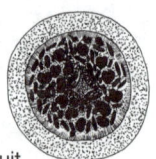

Inside of fruit

BANANA-FLAVOURED BUSH TOMATO
Solanum cleistogamum
Family: Solanaceae

SUB-SHRUB

Alyawarr	*mwanyem*
Anmatyerr	*mwanyem, manyem, alyelyek* (W. Anm.)
E. Arrernte	*lyelyake, mwanyeme*
Kaytetye	*mwanyeme, ngkwarlemaynteye*
Pintupi	*wiriny-wirrinypa*
Pitjantjatjara	*tjuntawara, wiluruwara, wiriny-wirinypa*
Warlpiri	*yipirntiri*

Spreading sub-shrub about 25 cm. **Leaves** soft, greyish to bluish-green. **Flowers** rather insignificant, pale purple or white. Mature **fruits** pale yellow, usually hidden under leaves. Recently named; confused with other species in past. Fruits produced a month or so after rain.

Habitat: Woodland. Most common with spinifex in sandy areas above salt lakes, but also occurs on creek levees and, in south-west, under mulga.

Uses: Fruit is a favoured food throughout area. The sweetest of all *Solanum* fruits, it often has a banana-like taste, and can be eaten when not fully ripe. Nutritional value is quite high, but large amounts can be collected only in particular favourable habitats: the fruits spoil quickly, or are eaten by animals. Some part of the plant is reputed to be used as a contraceptive (Pit.): unconfirmed.

Ref: *Bushfires & Bushtucker* p. 273

GREY BUSH TOMATO
Solanum coactiliferum
Family: Solanaceae

SUB-SHRUB

Alyawarr	*akatyerr*
E. Anmatyerr	*akatyerr*
W. Arrernte	*irtunpe*
Kaytetye	*arlkerre*
Pintupi	*it̲unypa, yit̲unypa*
Pitjantjatjara	*it̲unypa, kumpulpa, tjantu*
Warlpiri	*warrakarlu-karlu*

Erect clonal sub-shrub, about 35 cm. **Leaves** grey-green. **Flowers** purple. **Fruits** turn yellow at maturity; bone-like texture when dry. Usually has no thorns, but some are occasionally found on lower stems. Fruits generally produced whenever moisture conditions are suitable, but most often in warmer months.

Habitat: Spinifex sandplains and dune fields in the southern two thirds of the area.

Uses: One of the few Central Australian plant foods that is treated before being eaten (Pint., Pit., W. Arr.). Fruit is pounded between stones to squeeze out the bitter juices surrounding the seeds; water is sometimes added and the process repeated. The resultant paste is cooked then eaten. Children sometimes eat the fruit on the spot after carefully squeezing out the juice.

Ref: *Bushfires & Bushtucker* p. 274

NATIVE TOMATO, POTATO BUSH, WILD GOOSEBERRY
Solanum ellipticum
Family: Solanaceae

SUB-SHRUB

Alyawarr	*alperrantyey, ararnt*
E. Anmatyerr	*alperrantyey*
W. Anmatyerr	*ararnt*
E. Arrernte	*alperrantyeye, ararnte*
W. Arrernte	*rarnte*
Kaytetye	*alperrantyeye*
Pintupi	*wangki*
Pitjantjatjara	*kulypurpa, tawal-tawalpa, wangki, yuralpa*
Warlpiri	*wangki*

Spreading clonal sub-shrub about 30 cm. **Leaves** velvety grey or bluish-green. Attractive purple **flowers**. **Fruits** juicy; green with purplish stripes at first, becoming pale yellow when ripe. Fruits produced whenever moisture conditions suitable; severe frosts or heat can reduce crop.

Habitat: Most habitats, but commonest on foothills and lower hillslopes.

Uses: A traditional staple food plant throughout the area. Fruits spoil quickly after ripening, but relatively large amounts can be collected. Drought resistant: at least some fruits are produced during dry seasons. Europeans consider the fruit bitter but Aboriginal people eat them with gusto. Leaves are sometimes used as a substitute for pituri (Pit.).

Ref: *Bushfires & Bushtucker* p. 276

CLAY-SOIL BUSH TOMATO
Solanum esuriale
Family: Solanaceae

Erect clonal perennial about 25 cm. Generally thornless. **Leaves** narrow, grey-green. **Flowers** purple. Mature **fruits** pale yellow with rather rubbery texture. Fruit produced a month or more after rain.

Habitat: Only east of Alice Springs. Rare plant, found only in clayey soils.

Uses: Fruits are eaten by Alyawarr and Eastern Arrernte people. Abundant only in certain areas, so of limited importance as a food plant, but the fruits do keep well and are available late in the season.

Ref: *Bushfires & Bushtucker*
p. 278

DOG-EYE BUSH TOMATO, BONY-FRUITED BUSH TOMATO
Solanum quadriloculatum
Family: Solanaceae

Alyawarr	*arntek-arntek*
E. Anmatyerr	*arengkeylpart, arntek-arntek*
W. Anmatyerr	*arengkerlpart*
E. Arrernte	*akngwelye-alkngampelhe-ilenhe, arengke-alknge*
Kaytetye	*arengkalterrnhe, arengkalenye*
Pintupi	*warrakaḻu-kaḻu*
Pitjantjatjara	*rangki-rangki*
Warlpiri	*warrakarlu-karlu*

Clonal, erect sub-shrub about 35 cm. **Leaves** soft, grey-green, variable in size, drying to a yellowish colour. **Fruits** angular in shape, hard though somewhat spongy when green, drying to bone-like texture. *Fruits of this common plant are poisonous and should be avoided at all costs.* Frequently grows amongst edible *Solanum* species and is often mistaken for *S. ellipticum* (p. 75). *S. petrophilum*, another plant with poisonous fruit commonly found on hillsides, is usually given the same name as *S. quadriloculatum* and treated with the same caution.

Habitat: Throughout area in most habitats.

Uses: Not utilised.

Ref: *Bushfires & Bushtucker* p. 280

MUNGILYPA, CLAYPAN SAMPHIRE
Tecticornia verrucosa
Family: Chenopodiaceae

SUB-SHRUB

W. Anmatyerr	*akarnkwe*
Pintupi	*mungilypa*
Pitjantjatjara	*mungilypa*
Warlpiri	*mungilypa, mungulypa, warijangi, yapurnu* (?) (= salt lake)

Erect fleshy sub-shrub about 25 cm, grey-green to purplish green in colour. Peculiar plant with inconspicuous clustered **flowers** hidden in stem-like structures on upper ends of branches. Fleshy **'bulbs'** containing seeds occur at right angles to stem. Grows whenever moisture conditions suitable.

Habitat: Occurs sporadically west of longitude 132°; abundant only in extreme north-west of area, and only in fresh or semi-saline claypans.

Uses: An important food source for the Pintupi. Bulbs, often eaten directly from the plant, have a pleasant salty flavour. Seeds are easily separated from these structures, and are more usually ground into a paste and cooked on coals to form an unleavened bread. East of Lake Mackay this is often the principal traditional food when large groupings gather for important ceremonies.

Ref: *Bushfires & Bushtucker* p. 283

SHRUBS

VELVET HILL WATTLE
Acacia acradenia
Family: Mimosaceae

Alyawarr	*ampwey*
E. Anmatyerr	*ampwey*
Kaytetye	*ampweye*
Warlpiri	*ngardurrkura*

About 3 m high. **Leaves** broad, yellowish green. **Flowers** cylindrical, producing long, glabrous cylindrical **pods**, usually sparsely clustered. **Seeds** small, narrow, fairly soft coat. Seeds usually produced in October, dependent on rainfall. A relatively short-lived shrub which is killed by hot summer fires.

Habitat: Spinifex hills. Never very common, but found on scree slopes of hills in northern and western areas.

Uses: Seeds and gum eaten (Aly'rr, Warl.) Walpiri use trunks for spears.

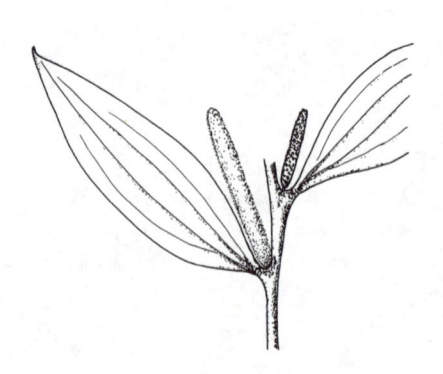

Ref: *Bushfires & Bushtucker* p. 85

WHIPSTICK WATTLE
Acacia adsurgens
Family: Mimosaceae

Alyawarr	*ilwerreny*
E. Anmatyerr	*antyweleny, ilwerreny (?), ateyepenh (?)*
Kaytetye	*antywelenye*
Warlpiri	*mirntirlpiri, minyana, kulaki, puju-parnta*

Rigid shrub to 3 m. **Leaves** narrow. **Flower spikes** cylindrical. **Pods** narrow, densely clustered. **Seeds** small, narrow, soft coat. Short-lived. Seed usually produced in late spring, depending on rainfall. *A. tenuissima* is similar, with cylindrical leaves and thin-coated seeds with a distinct yellow aril.

Habitat: Often common on spinifex sand plains; also found on gravelly scree slopes in northern third of area.

Uses: Seeds eaten (Aly'rr, Anm'rr, Warl.). Warlpiri people use the leaves for medicinal purposes: boiled to use as a wash for general complaints, or used to smoke babies as a treatment for diarrhoea.

Ref: *Bushfires & Bushtucker* p. 86

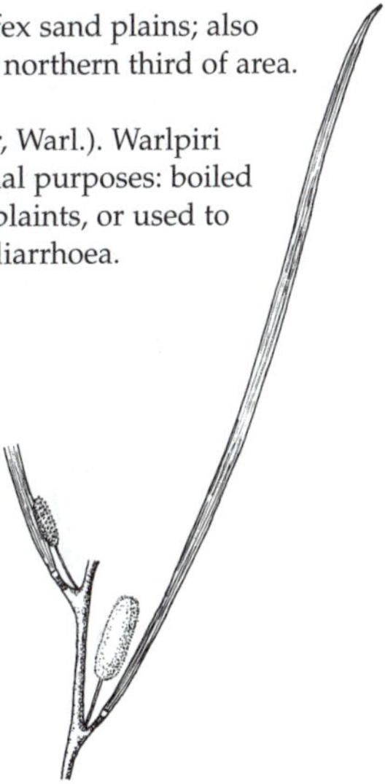

PIRRARU, SHINY-LEAVED WATTLE
Acacia ancistrocarpa
Family: Mimosaceae

Alyawarr	*irrar*
E. Anmatyerr	*irrar*
Kaytetye	*perrare*
Warlpiri	*pirraru, wartarurru*

Rigid shrub to 2.5 m. **Leaves** shiny. **Flower spikes** cylindrical. **Pods** broad, becoming incurved when dry. **Seeds** small, narrow, soft coat: produced in late spring and forcibly ejected from pods when dry.

Habitat: Spinifex sandplains and sandhills, spinifex hills. Occurs in northern third of area, usually in better-watered portions.

Uses: Seeds are reputedly eaten (Warl.), usually being gathered from around ants' nests. Leaves are used to smoke babies as a treatment for diarrhoea.

Ref: *Bushfires & Bushtucker* p. 87

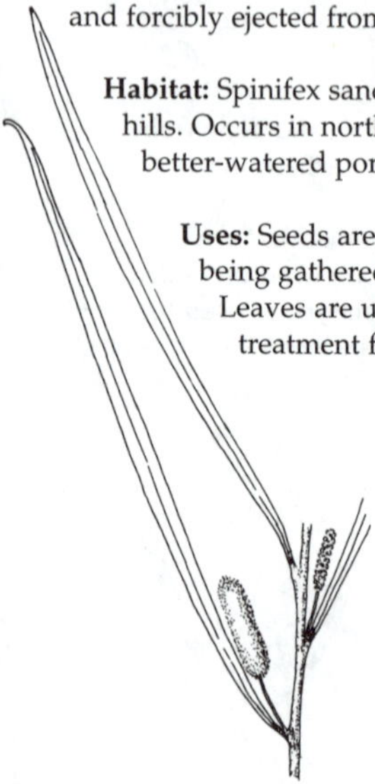

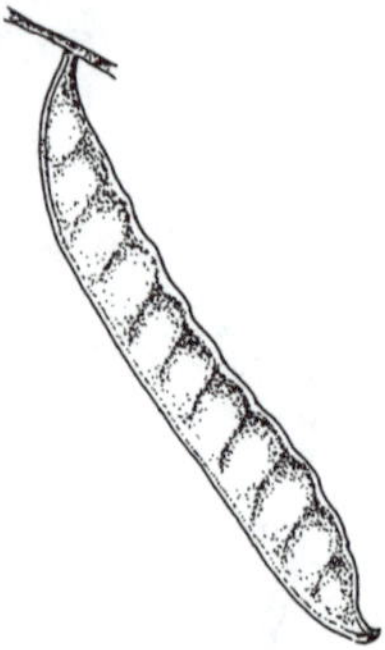

SICKLE-LEAVED WATTLES
Acacia cowleana and *A. elachantha*
Family: Mimosaceae

Alyawarr	*alerrey*
E. Anmatyerr	*ilkert*
W. Anmatyerr	*alkart*
Kaytetye	*elkerte*
Pintupi	*kilkiti*
Warlpiri	*kalkardi, kanarlarrampi, parrapi*

Up to 7 m. **Bark** smooth. **Leaves** large, sickle-shaped. **Flower spikes** cylindrical. **Pods** long, thin, densely clustered. **Seeds** small, soft-coated with rather large red aril. Aboriginal people do not distinguish between the two species. *A. colei* is similar, but leaves are silvery, less curved.

Habitat: Spinifex sandhills and sand plains, in watercourses or better-watered spinifex areas. *Acacia cowleana* is also found in the Macdonnell Ranges, only in sheltered areas above the frost line.

Uses: Seed is eaten. Harbours edible grubs and honey-producing scale.

Ref: *Bushfires & Bushtucker* p. 94 and *A. colei*: *Bushfires & Bushtucker* p. 92

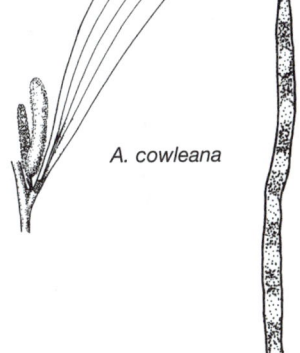

A. cowleana

SILVER WITCHETTY
Acacia cuthbertsonii
Family: Mimosaceae

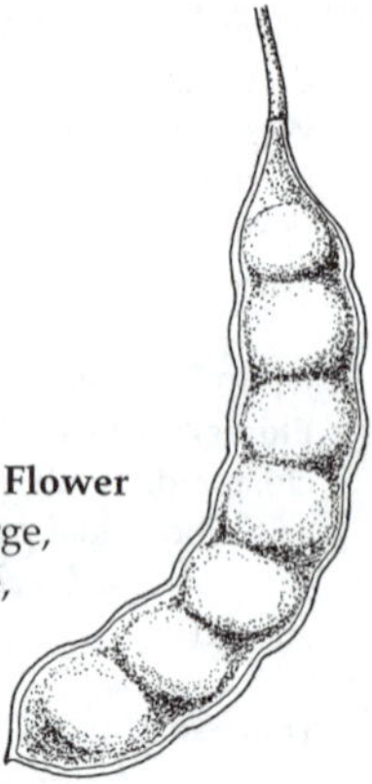

Alyawarr	*irley, pirley*
E. Anmatyerr	*peyley*
W. Anmatyerr	*perley*
Kaytetye	*peyleye*
Pintupi	*pi̱liyi, yalpirri*
Pitjantjatjara	*alpiri, apulya, kalirma*
Warlpiri	*pirliyi*

Rounded shrub to 3 m. **Leaves** silvery. **Flower spikes** cylindrical. **Pods** distinctive: large, glossy, swollen over seeds. **Seeds** large, hard coated.

Habitat: Rare in Macdonnell Ranges. Elsewhere, sporadic on gravelly hills or near small watercourses.

Uses: Green seeds are cooked in the pod and eaten. Only the Pintupi are reputed to use the dry seeds. Inner bark is used as a bandage and gives fibre for rope, sandals etc. (Warl., Pin.).

Ref: *Bushfires & Bushtucker* p. 95

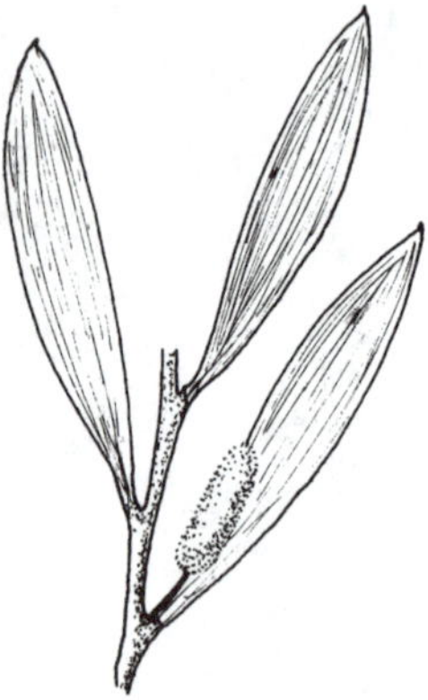

MIMOSA BUSH
Acacia farnesiana
Family: Mimosaceae

SHRUB

Alyawarr	*alekw, alwek*
Anmatyerr	*alekw, irnker* (W. Anm.?)
E. Arrernte	*arlakwe*
W. Arrernte	*irlakwe*
Warlpiri	*yintirningirningi, putunarri*

3–5 m. **Bark** smooth. **Leaves** fern-like, strong spine at base. **Flowers** pale, developing into thick cylindrical **pods**. **Seeds** large, sub-globular, hard-coated; produced late autumn or early summer.

Habitat: Restricted to clayey soils, usually near watercourses. Rarely abundant.

Uses: Seed is generally not eaten. Wood is used for axe handles, music sticks etc. Leaf spines are useful for removing splinters. In other parts of the world, flowers are used to produce a base for perfumes, and medicinal properties are attributed to the bark.

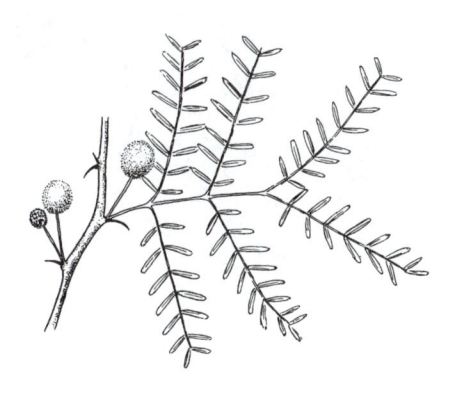

Ref: *Bushfires & Bushtucker* p. 99

FIRE WATTLE, ODD-LEAF WATTLE
Acacia inaequilatera
Family: Mimosaceae

Alyawarr	*ngart, rtwamel*
Warlpiri	*janjinki, janjirnngi*

Erect, sparsely branched shrub about 3 m. **Bark** corky. **Leaves** bluish-green, triangular, ending in stiff spine; spines also occur on **branches**. **Flower spikes** globular. **Pods** curved.

Habitat: Spinifex sandplains and sandhills, spinifex hills: always found with spinifex in deep red sand or on gravelly scree slopes. Common in previous mulga areas recently invaded by spinifex.

Uses: Seeds are reputedly eaten (Warl.). Elsewhere in Australia, the red bast under the bark is used to treat sores.

Ref: *Bushfires & Bushtucker* p. 101

WITCHETTY BUSH
Acacia kempeana
Family: Mimosaceae

Alyawarr	*atnyem*
E. Anmatyerr	*atnyem, anyem*
W. Anmatyerr	*anyem*
E. Arrernte	*atnyeme*
W. Arrernte	*tnyeme*
Kaytetye	*atnyeme*
Pintupi	*ilykuwarra, iripili, piya<u>n</u>pa, yilykuwarra*
Pitjantjatjara	*ilykuwara, yilykuwara*
Warlpiri	*ngarlkirdi, yiripili*

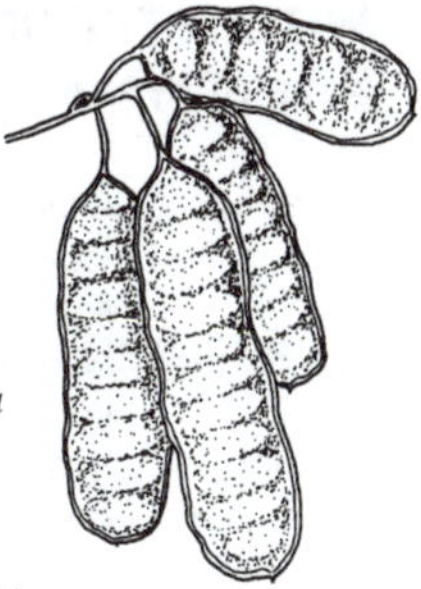

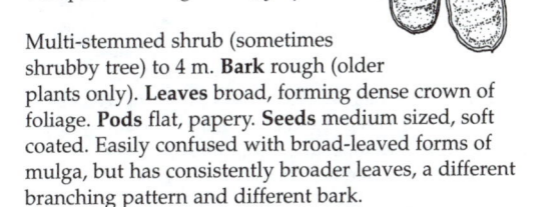

Multi-stemmed shrub (sometimes shrubby tree) to 4 m. **Bark** rough (older plants only). **Leaves** broad, forming dense crown of foliage. **Pods** flat, papery. **Seeds** medium sized, soft coated. Easily confused with broad-leaved forms of mulga, but has consistently broader leaves, a different branching pattern and different bark.

Habitat: Widespread throughout region; most common on foothills and in limestone areas.

Uses: Seed is an important food, usually treated like mulga seed. Red lerp scale (see *A. aneura*, p. 150) is commonly found on this plant. Stems and roots are used as fighting spears or fish spears (S. Arr.). The wood may be used as a substitute when mulga wood is unavailable. The leaves and inner bark from the roots have medicinal uses. A very important plant in Central Australia because of the large tasty grubs found in its roots.

Ref: *Bushfires & Bushtucker* p. 102

WITCHETTY GRUB
larva of *Xyleutes biarpiti*

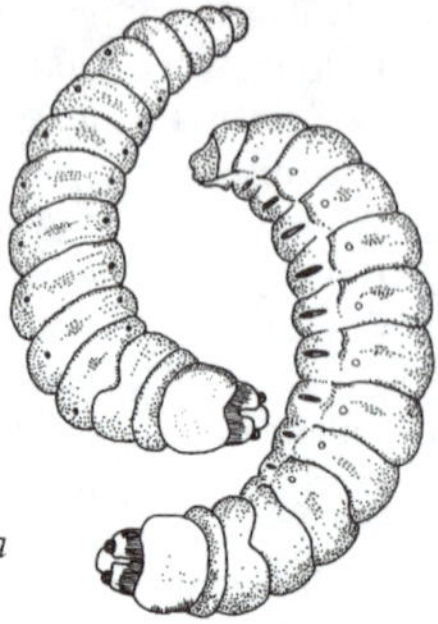

Alyawarr	*atnyemayt*
Anmatyerr	*tnyematy, atnyemayt, anyemayt*
E. Arrernte	*atnyematye*
Kaytetye	*atnyemayte*
Pintupi	*lunki, maku, pila<u>n</u>pa*
Pitjantjatjara	*lunki, maku ilykuwarra*
Warlpiri	*ngarlkirdi*

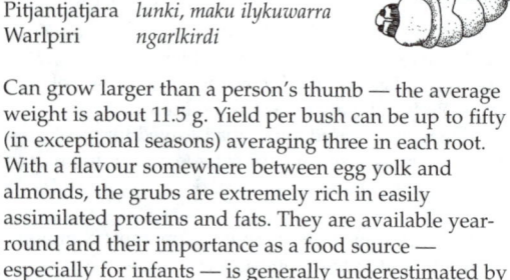

Can grow larger than a person's thumb — the average weight is about 11.5 g. Yield per bush can be up to fifty (in exceptional seasons) averaging three in each root. With a flavour somewhere between egg yolk and almonds, the grubs are extremely rich in easily assimilated proteins and fats. They are available year-round and their importance as a food source — especially for infants — is generally underestimated by non-Aboriginal people. The moths are also eaten.

Ref: *Bushfires & Bushtucker* p. 103

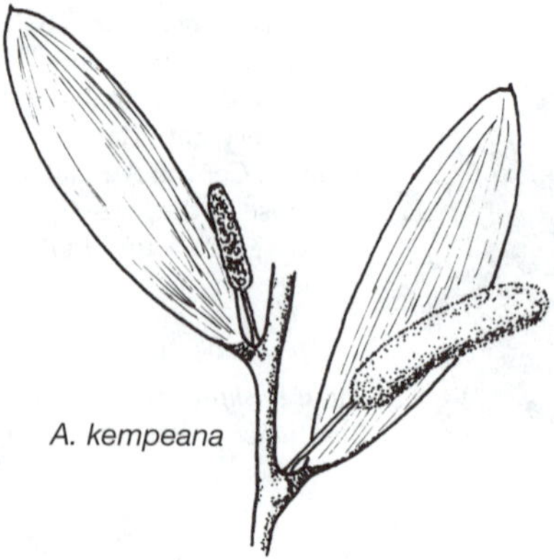

A. kempeana

UMBRELLA BUSH
Acacia ligulata
Family: Mimosaceae

Alyawarr	arterrk
Anmatyerr	rterrk, arterrk
E. Arrernte	arterrke
W. Arrernte	irterrke
Kaytetye	arterrke
Pintupi	nyukurrka (?), wa̱tarrka
Pitjantjatjara	wa̱tarka
Warlpiri	wardarrka

Shrub to 2.5 m, usually with rounded shape. **Bark** rough only when very old. Variable **leaf** shape. **Pods** hard, fracture between seeds when mature. **Seeds** medium sized, hard, with scarlet or yellow aril: usually available in September, although flowering and seed production depend on rainfall.

Habitat: Spinifex sandhills and sandplains, limestone communities, near salt lakes or in red sand. Always with spinifex.

Uses: Seeds are eaten consistently only by the Pintupi and Pitjantjatjara, because of the effort involved in collection. Gum seeping from the trunk and grubs in the roots are used by all groups. Ash is used for pituri. Medicinal smoke from the leaves is used for a range of illnesses (Warl.). A medicinal wash is made from a decoction of the bark (Aly'rr).

Ref: *Bushfires & Bushtucker* p. 105

SHRUB

TURPENTINE BUSH
Acacia lysiphloia
Family: Mimosaceae

Alyawarr	*menyempwer, merlerr*
E. Anmatyerr	*irrtnyengirrtny*
Kaytetye	*menyempere*
Warlpiri	*murlurrpa*

About 2 m. Characteristic red **bark** which curls on trunk. **Leaves** small, flat, dark green; sticky when young. **Pods** sticky; **seeds** small, hard, yellow aril. *A. monticola* is similar but has globular flower spikes and broader greyish-green leaves.

Habitat: Spinifex hills: gravelly outcrops, flats fringing watercourses and woodland.

Uses: A powerful medicinal plant: used to smoke newborn babies and mothers, and sick babies in general. Can be used to make an infusion for itchy skin. Seeds are said to be eaten.

Ref: *Bushfires & Bushtucker* p. 106

SPINY-LEAVED WATTLE, STIFF WATTLE
Acacia maitlandii
Family: Mimosaceae

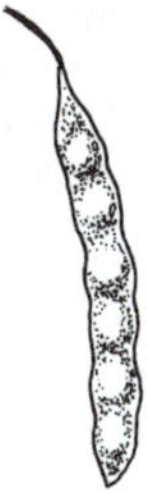

Alyawarr	*aleperlterrk*
E. Anmatyerr	*arleperlterrk*
W. Arrernte	*lwepe-lwepe*
Kaytetye	*arleperlterrke*
Pitjantjatjara	*kurutanpa, kuwiyuturuturu, ngarkalya*
Warlpiri	*kurdurrurdururru*

A sparsely branched shrub about 2 m high. **Leaves** small, stiff; sharp spine at tip. **Flower spikes** small, globular. **Pods** small, narrow, papery. **Seeds** rounded, small, soft. Flowers after rain except in mid-summer.

Habitat: Found with spinifex, on sandplains and dunes or on rocky hillsides.

Uses: Arandic peoples probably eat the seeds; Warlpiri people definitely do not; there is conflicting information regarding the Pitjantjatjara. Grubs in the roots are eaten and the wood is sometimes used for spears.

Ref: *Bushfires & Bushtucker* p. 107

WAXY WATTLE
Acacia melleodora
Family: Mimosaceae

Alyawarr	*alhanker, alhepalh*
E. Anmatyerr	*ilkwenarr, alhepalh*
W. Anmatyerr	*lkwernarr, patwet*
S. Arrernte	*ilpakilparre*
Kaytetye	*alhepalhe, arewelarre*
Pintupi	*minytju, mulyati, utjanypa, yurrtjanpa, lungkunpa* (fruit)
Pitjantjatjara	*mintju, mulyati, ngarkalya*
Warlpiri	*matutu, marlarntarrpa, patutu, pilpirrinpa, wurrpardi*

Sparsely branched shrub about 2.5 m. **Leaves** green, sticky (new growth) appearing grey-green as sticky substance dries to a whitish crust. **Pods** wide, papery. **Seeds** small, brown with soft coat; usually produced during late autumn or early summer: crop usually prolific.

Habitat: Spinifex sandplains and sandhills, spinifex hills: in deep red sand or on quartzite hills, but always with spinifex. The similar *A. dictyophleba* is found only in the Simpson Desert.

Uses: Seeds are an important food; grubs are found in the roots. Leaves are used to smoke mothers and newborn children, and young women at the onset of menses (Warl.). The wood is sometimes used for spears, but only occasional plants have straight enough trunks. (This form is often called *A. jensenii*.)

Ref: *Bushfires & Bushtucker* p. 96 (as *A. dictyophleba*)

Top: *Triodia pungens* (soft spinifex)
Right: Heating the ants' nest to obtain adhesive
Bottom: Moulding the hot adhesive

Top: *Panicum decompositum* (native millet)
Bottom: *Yakirra australiensis* (desert Flinders grass)

Top: *Pterocaulon serrulatum* (apple bush)
Bottom: *Stemodia viscosa* (pintye-pintye, sweet pillow)

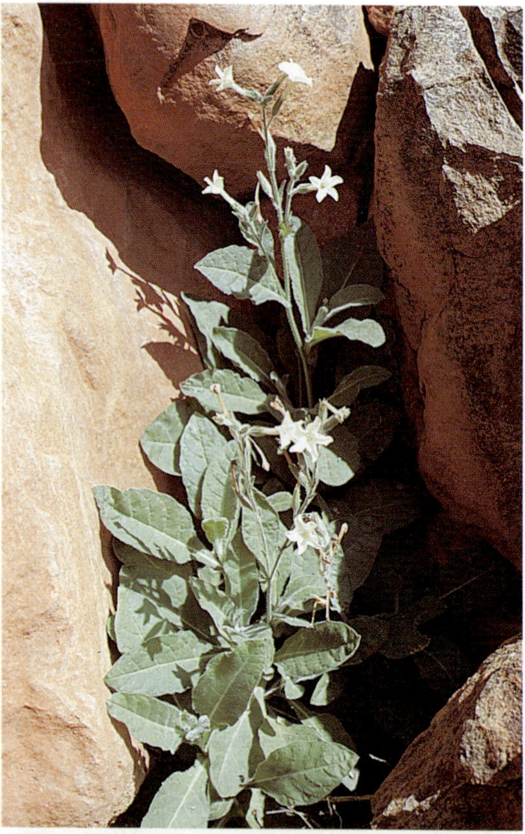

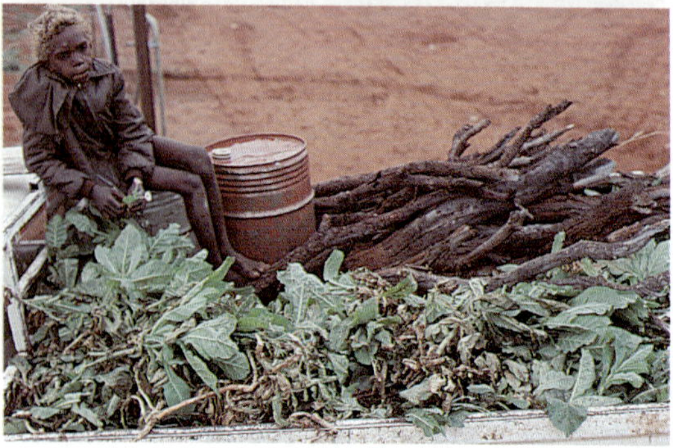

Top left: *Nicotiana gossei* (rock pituri)
Bottom left: A truck loaded with *Nicotiana gossei*
Top right: A field of *Nicotiana excelsior* in the Mann Range
Bottom right: *Nicotiana excelsior* (shiny-leaved native tobacco)

Top: *Solanum centrale* (desert raisin) showing fruit and flower
Centre: Gathering *Solanum centrale* on a roadside
Bottom: Ripe desert raisins

Top: *Solanum chippendalei* (bush tomato)
Bottom: The fruit of the bush tomato

Top: *Eremophila freelingii* (hill fuschia)
Right: *Prostanthera striatiflora* (mint bush)
Bottom: *Ficus platypoda* (wild fig)

DESERT MULGA
Acacia minyura
Family: Mimosaceae

Pitjantjatjara *puyukara, minyura*

Rounded shrub, about 2.5 m. **Leaves** sticky when young, grey-green when mature. **Pods** short, sometimes almost circular. Flowering and fruiting habits similar to typical mulga.

Habitat: Sandy soils, often with spinifex. Often found fringing stands of true mulga in between dunes, growing in the sandier soils.

Uses: Mulga apples are commonly found on this bush, but have an unpleasant bitter aftertaste. The grey granular resin covering most of the leaves and twigs is used as a cementing agent in the south-east corner of the area, where the more favoured *Triodia pungens* (p. 27) is unavailable. Branches are placed on a hard surface and beaten with a stick. Fragments falling to the bottom are gathered, cleaned and then melted by passing a burning stick over them. Ashes are added for extra strength. The resultant black mass does not have the strength of resin from *Triodia* but is suitable for most purposes.

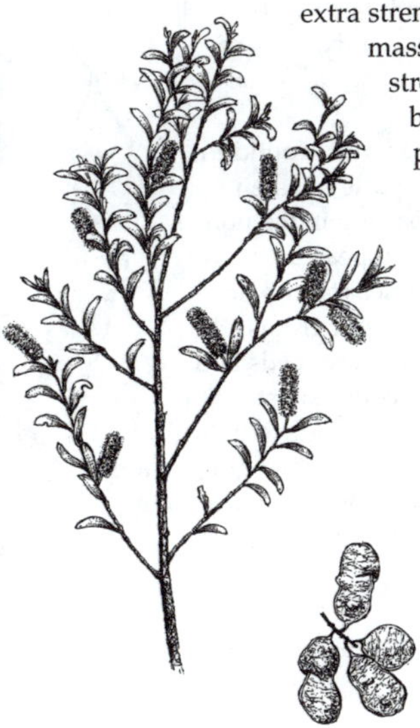

Ref: *Bushfires & Bushtucker* p. 108

COLONY WATTLE
Acacia murrayana
Family: Mimosaceae

Alyawarr	*arrely*
Anmatyerr	*arrely*
E. Arrernte	*arnterre, arrelye*
W. Arrernte	*irrelye*
Kaytetye	*arrelye*
Pintupi	*nyurrinpa*
Pitjantjatjara	*tjuntala, tjuntjula*
Warlpiri	*juntala*

Clonal shrub about 3 m. **Bark** usually smooth, white. **Flowers** bright golden yellow. **Pods** flat, each seed is clearly defined. **Seeds** have a hard, thick coat. Flowers only in spring; seeds are produced in early summer.

Habitat: Spinifex sandplains and sandhills. Rare north of Alice Springs; absent in far north. Most common on sandplains and dune fields, but extends into sandy areas of other habitats.

Uses: Seeds are roasted and ground to make an edible paste or eaten green after roasting in the pod. (Early European settlers sometimes roasted or burnt and ground the mature seeds as a coffee substitute.) Harbours edible grubs. Edible white gum exudes from insect damage in the trunk.

Ref: *Bushfires & Bushtucker* p. 110

HORSE MULGA, PENCIL WATTLE
Acacia ramulosa
Family: Mimosaceae

Pitjantjatjara *pakuta, palpa*

Rounded shrub about 2.5 m, similar appearance to mulga. **Leaves** upright, bluish-green. Characteristic grey, brown-striped **pods** are almost pencil-shaped when mature, and hang like Christmas tree decorations!

Habitat: Grows in sandy areas, often on sand dunes, in sand overtopping limestone or near salt lakes, sometimes with or near mulga. Common south of latitude 22° but not found close to Musgrave or Macdonnell ranges.

Uses: Seed of this plant is eaten; other parts are almost certainly used in the same way as mulga (p. 150).

Ref: *Bushfires & Bushtucker* p. 115

KURAPUKA, SCRUB WATTLE
Acacia stipuligera
Family: Mimosaceae

Alyawarr	*ampwey*
E. Anmatyerr	*ampwey*
Kayteye	*ampweye*
Pintupi	*tjirrpirinypa, wilpurra*
Warlpiri	*ngirnti-yirrpi, jirrpirinypa, kurapuka*

2–3 m high. **Leaves** broad, dull green. **Flower spikes** cylindrical, producing long, hairy, cylindrical **pods**, densely clustered. **Seeds** small, narrow and soft coated. Very similar to *A. acradenia* (p. 80), and often given same Aboriginal name. Quick growing and short lived.

Habitat: Restricted to spinifex sandplains and dunes. Often forms thick scrubs in better-watered areas and at base of dunes.

Uses: Seeds are pounded and eaten. Gum is also edible.

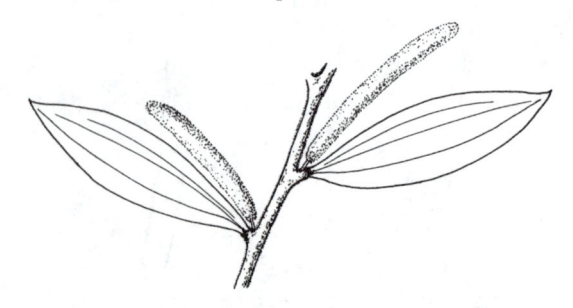

Ref: *Bushfires & Bushtucker* p. 117

DEAD FINISH
Acacia tetragonophylla
Family: Mimosaceae

Alyawarr	*arlketyerr*
Anmatyerr	*arlketyerr, tyer* (W.Anm.)
E. Arrernte	*arlketyerre*
W. Arrernte	*irlketyerre*
Kayteye	*arlketyerre*
Pintupi	*wakalpuka*
Pitjantjatjara	*kuṟungantiṟi, wakalpuka, lungkunpa* (ground seed)
Warlpiri	*kurarra*

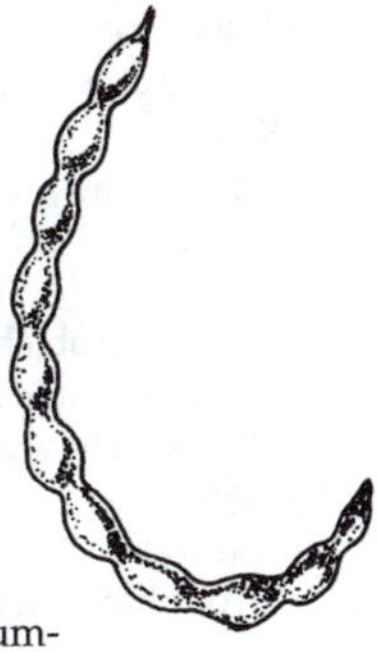

Loosely branched shrub to 3 m. **Leaves** narrow, sharp-pointed, clustered on branches. **Flower spikes** globular, scattered. **Pods** thin, curved. **Seeds** medium-sized, soft with large yellow or red aril, usually produced in autumn but not in large numbers.

Habitat: Non-spinifex hills, woodland. Scattered throughout area, usually found in non-sandy habitats, especially low hills. More common in the Musgrave Ranges.

Uses: Seeds are usually eaten green after being cooked in the pod. Edible grubs are found in the roots. Wood is hard, finely grained and suitable for artefacts (it was favoured by early European settlers for whip handles). Sharp points on the leaves remove warts (Pit.); the infusion from the root bark is used to treat cuts and sores. A favoured nesting site for finches, and droppings in abandoned nests have important medicinal properties.

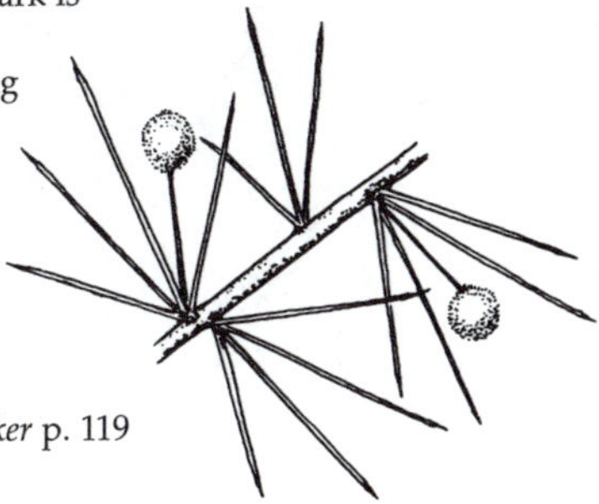

Ref: *Bushfires & Bushtucker* p. 119

BLUE WATTLE, LEATHER-LEAVED COLONY WATTLE
Acacia validinervia
Family: Mimosaceae

Alyawarr	*ilyarn, ilyarnayt*
Anmatyerr	*ilyarnayt, larnayt, iylarn* (E. Anm.)
Kaytetye	*eylanayte, lanayte*
Pitjantjatjara	*alumaru, nyala-nyala*
Warlpiri	*karlurnturrngu*

Clonal shrub about 1.5 m. **Bark** smooth white or pinkish. **Leaves** bluish-green, thick and leathery. **Flowers** showy, golden yellow.

Habitat: With spinifex, on sandplains or hillsides throughout area.

Uses: One of the few common acacias whose seed is never eaten. Favoured, however, for edible grubs found in the roots.

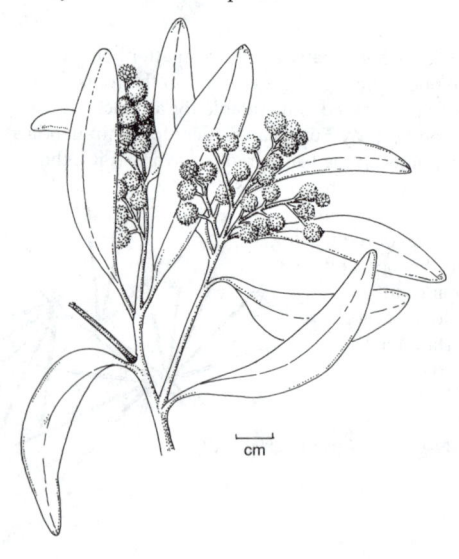

Ref: *Bushfires & Bushtucker* p. 120

ACACIA BUSH, ELEGANT ACACIA
Acacia victoriae
Family: Mimosaceae

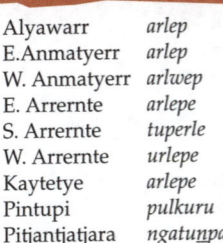

SHRUB

Alyawarr	*arlep*
E. Anmatyerr	*arlep*
W. Anmatyerr	*arlwep*
E. Arrernte	*arlepe*
S. Arrernte	*tuperle*
W. Arrernte	*urlepe*
Kaytetye	*arlepe*
Pintupi	*pulkuru*
Pitjantjatjara	*ngatunpa, aliti*
Warlpiri	*kanaparlku, yalupu, yarlirti*

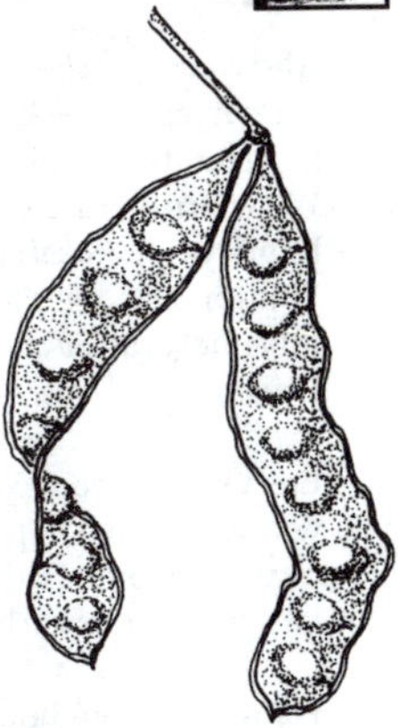

Many-branched shrub or small tree up to 5 m. **Leaves** green or grey-green. May be **thorns** on branches of adult shrubs. **Flowers** globular, pale yellow. **Pods** papery; flat until seeds formed, then becoming distended around seeds. **Seeds** medium-sized, rounded, hard with a thick coat. Flowers only in spring; seeds are usually shed in early summer but may hang on the bush for some time.

Habitat: Most common on river flats (often forms thick scrubs); also found in limestone and saline areas.

Uses: Important food in the central area. Seeds are roasted in the pods when fully formed but still green; hard-coated mature seeds are ground. The trunk exudes edible white gum; edible grubs may be found in the roots and trunk of mature plants. The wood is sometimes used for the blades of hunting spears.

Ref: *Bushfires & Bushtucker* p. 121

NATIVE CURRANT, NATIVE CITRUS
Canthium latifolium
Family: Rubiaceae

Alyawarr	*ahakey, arrarntenh, artapaly*
Anmatyerr	*ahakey, artapaly, arrarntenh*
E. Arrernte	*ahakeye, arrarntenhe*
W. Arrernte	*akeye, tnemetneme*
Kaytetye	*ahakeye*
Pintupi	*awalyurru, tatupirrpa, yawalyurru*
Pitjantjatjara	*awalyuru, wanakatakata*
Warlpiri	*yaakiyi, yawakiyi, yarrarntinyi, yawalyurru*

Erect shrub about 3 m. **Leaves** broad, stiff, deep green with citrus-like appearance. Small white **flowers** usually inconspicuous. **Fruit** ripen to a black colour. Fruits in late summer or early winter, depending on rainfall.

Habitat: Throughout area, with mulga or fringing spinifex stands, on sandplains and hills.

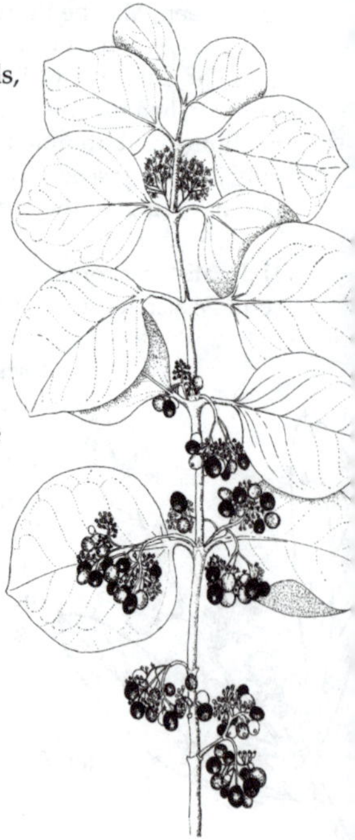

Uses: The small, sweet, black berries are a favoured food throughout the area, even though much of their bulk consists of inedible seed. They produce a burning rash on the lips and tongue if eaten in large quantities. Dry berries survive for considerable periods and are collected and reconstituted in water. An important plant in Aboriginal mythology.

C. attenuatum

Alyawarr	*yernt*
E. Anmatyerr	*yernt*
Kaytetye	*yernte*

Similar, but with narrow leaf.

Ref: *Bushfires & Bushtucker* p. 136

MULGA NATIVE CURRANT
NARROW-LEAVED NATIVE CURRANT
Canthium lineare
Family: Rubiaceae

SHRUB

Alyawarr	*ateylp*
Anmatyerr	*ngkwernelyerr, ngkwernateylp* (E. Anm.)
E. Arrernte	*ngkwernelyerre*
Kaytetye	*ateylpe, ngkwernateylpe*
Pintupi	*wanakatakata*
Warlpiri	*wakuwarlpa, yuwirnti, yiwirnti*

Similar to native currant except for narrow **leaves**.

Habitat: Occurs (only occasionally) in thick mulga scrubs, more or less throughout area.

Uses: The plant is fairly rare, so although the berries are eaten, they are not a very important part of a traditional diet.

Ref: *Bushfires & Bushtucker* p. 137

SHRUB

SPLIT-JACK
Capparis lasiantha
Family: Capparaceae

Alyawarr	*altwerr, ampwerlp*
Anmatyerr	*alwerr*
E. Arrernte	*alurre*
Kaytetye	*alwerre*
Pintupi	*yin̠turinka (?)*
Warlpiri	*papilyi, papingi, yarrunungu, yinturringa*

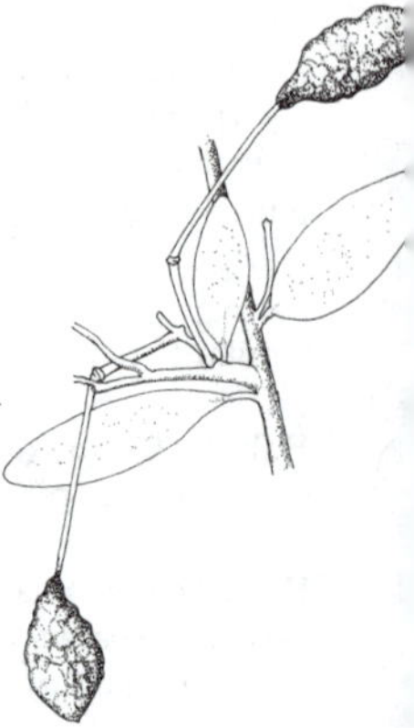

Shrubby vine with hooked **thorns** and zigzag growth form. **Leaves** have brown tinge. **Flowers** white, small. **Fruit** oval with yellow pulp, brown **seeds**; splits when ripe. Fruits in summer months.

Habitat: Rare; found on rocky (spinifex) hillsides or in woodland below, in the northern half of the area.

Uses: A favoured fruit wherever it occurs. Only the pulp is eaten. Immature fruit is often buried in sand or otherwise stored until it ripens. Has medicinal uses in other parts of Australia.

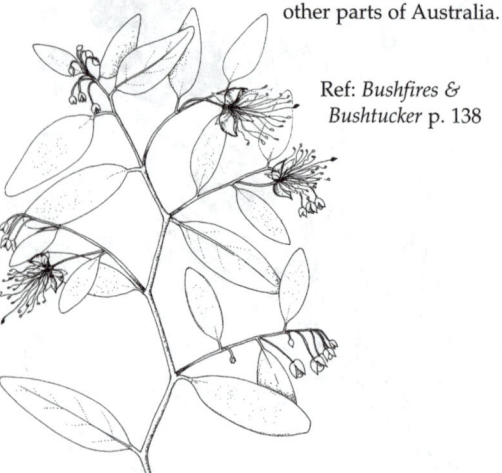

Ref: *Bushfires & Bushtucker* p. 138

GIDGEE WILD ORANGE, NARROW-LEAF BUMBLE
Capparis loranthifolia
Family: Capparaceae

Alyawarr	*angerterrk*
Anmatyerr	*iwerrarrkw*
Kaytetye	*angerterrke*

Rigid shrub to 3 m. **Bark** rough. **Flowers** creamy. Fruit are usually produced in summer.

Habitat: Woodland; often grows near watercourses or with gidgee. Rare in northern half of area.

Uses: The pulp of the fruit is eaten.

Ref: *Bushfires & Bushtucker* p. 139

WILD ORANGE
Capparis mitchellii
Family: Capparaceae

Alyawarr	*atwakey*
Anmatyerr	*atwakey, atakwey*
E. Arrernte	*atwakeye*
W. Arrernte	*mpeltyarte*
Kaytetye	*atwakeye*
Pintupi	*umpultjati, yumpultjati*
Pitjantjatjara	*umpultjati, tjawili* (?)
Warlpiri	*watakiyi*

Small compact tree about 3.5 m. **Leaves** dark green, leathery. **Flowers** creamy white; open at night and wither before end of next day. **Fruit** yellow-green when ripe with characteristic pleasant odour. **Pulp** yellow. Juvenile plants look quite different from adult tree: with small, sparse **leaves** and tangled **branches** which are vine-like and extremely thorny. New growth on adult trees after fire or grazing is similar. Fruit usually ripens October–January if conditions are favourable.

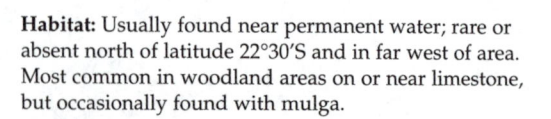

Habitat: Usually found near permanent water; rare or absent north of latitude 22°30'S and in far west of area. Most common in woodland areas on or near limestone, but occasionally found with mulga.

Uses: An important food in the central area; the rich, pleasant taste gives way to a less appealing kerosene aftertaste. Arrernte people use the thorny juvenile branches to catch bats in caves. In other parts of Australia the bark is used medicinally.

Ref: *Bushfires & Bushtucker* p. 139

WILD PASSIONFRUIT, CAPER BUSH
Capparis spinosa var. *nummularia*
Family: Capparaceae

Alyawarr	*arrwerneng*
Anmatyerr	*arrwetneng, arrweneng*
E. Arrernte	*arrutnenge*
W. Arrernte	*rratninge*
Kaytetye	*arrwetnenge*
Pintupi	*uraningi* (?)
Warlpiri	*mingkilyananga*

Spiny shrub about 1.5 m high, 2–3 m diameter. **Flowers** white, delicate, open at night and last only a day or two. **Fruits** green, inconspicuous until they ripen, then quickly turn yellow and usually split open. **Seeds** bitter, black. Edible **pulp** yellow. Fruit ripen in summer and often last until first frosts.

Habitat: Woodland, limestone communities, on river flats or low calcareous hills; usually under trees or in sheltered areas.

Uses: The fruit is eaten throughout the plant's range. Ants and birds are attracted to the ripe fruit; humans pick them green to ripen off the bush. Elsewhere in the world a different variety is used medicinally and the flower buds (capers) are eaten.

Ref: *Bushfires & Bushtucker* p. 141

NORTHERN WILD ORANGE
Capparis umbonata
Family: Capparaceae

Alyawarr	*akarley*
Anmatyerr	*akarlety*
Arrernte	*akarletye*
Kaytetye	*akarletye*
Warlpiri	*jukurru, ngarntajari, jalipana*

Shrub or small slender tree about 3.5 m. Rough, dark **bark**. Weeping **foliage**. **Flowers** white, attractive and fragile. **Fruits** hang down on long stalks, turn yellow or reddish at maturity. Juvenile growth similar to *C. mitchellii* (p. 112). Fruit most often ripen during February.

Habitat: North of latitude 22°30'S only. Wide variety of habitats, but most common on river flats.

Uses: Aboriginal people generally consider the fruit to be better than other wild oranges. Green fruit is often ripened in hot sand. A decoction from this plant is used as a medicinal wash in other parts of Australia.

Ref: *Bushfires & Bushtucker* p. 142

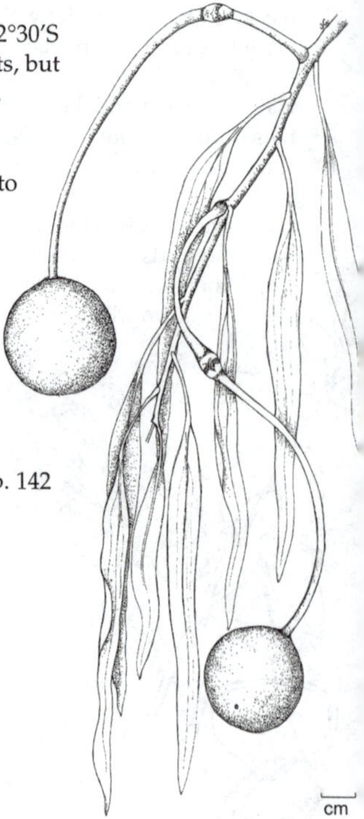

cm

CONKLEBERRY, CONKERBERRY
Carissa lanceolata
Family: Apocynaceae

SHRUB

Alyawarr	*anwekety, arnwekety*
Anmatyerr	*aperlap, arnwekety, arnekwety*
E. Arrernte	*aperlape*
W. Arrernte	*irneketye, larletye*
Kaytetye	*arnewetye, perlape, anweketye*
Pintupi	*nganangu, ngamunypurru*
Warlpiri	*kupurturru, marnakiji, marnikiji, marningiji, marnunguju*

Tangled, spiny shrub to 2 m. **Flowers** fragrant, white. **Berry** black; contains two small knobbly **seeds**. Flowers after rain.

Habitat: Most common north of Alice Springs. Generally found in woodland communities.

Uses: The berries are sweet and are favoured wherever this shrub is found, but if consumed in large quantities they make one thirsty. Berries are only available on the bush for a few weeks, but dried berries are often gathered from the ground and soaked before being eaten. The finely grained wood is used for spear heads. Orange inner bark from the roots is soaked in water and the solution used as a medicinal wash, particularly for skin and eye conditions. Thorns are used to cure warts.

Ref: *Bushfires & Bushtucker* p. 143

SMOOTH SPIDERBUSH
Clerodendrum floribundum
Family: Verbenaceae

POISONOUS

Alyawarr	arrngern
Anmatyerr	arlkwerrkng, tywerlp, arrkngern
E. Arrernte	arrkngerne
W. Arrernte	irremarte
Kaytetye	arrkngerne
Pintupi	tatupitji, yirimarri
Warlpiri	jatipiji, jatupiji, punayi, wijilypi, yirdimardi, yirimardi

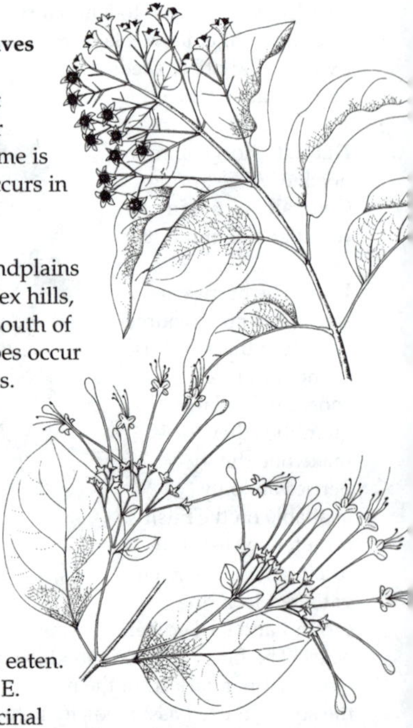

About 2 m high. **Leaves** stiff, bright green. **Flowers** white. **Fruit** small, fleshy, pink or purple. Flowering time is variable but often occurs in summer months.

Habitat: Spinifex sandplains and sandhills, spinifex hills, watercourses. Rare south of Alice Springs but does occur in Petermann Ranges.

Uses: Roots are eaten in hard times: they are cooked in hot sand, the bark is removed and the root is smashed on a stone. All but the fibrous parts are eaten. Fruits are *not* eaten. E. Warlpiri use a medicinal decoction of the leaves. Elsewhere in Australia, the leaves are sometimes used as a substitute for pituri and a decoction of the wood is drunk for aches and pains.

Ref: *Bushfires & Bushtucker* p. 149

Top: Fruit of *Capparis spinosa* var. *nummularia* (wild passionfruit)
Right: Fruit of *Capparis loranthifolia* (gidgee wild orange)
Bottom: Wild passionfruit bush in flower

Top: *Eremophila longifolia* (emu bush)
Bottom: *Hakea leucoptera* (needlewood) flowering

Top: *Grevillea juncifolia* (honey grevillea)
Bottom: *Grevillea eriostachya* (bird flower grevillea)

Top: Digging for witchetty grubs
Centre: A witchetty grub still in the root
Bottom left: *Acacia kempeana* (witchetty bush)
Bottom right: Witchetty bush seed

Top: Yandying mulga seed (*Acacia aneura*)
Right: *Acacia victoriae* (acacia bush) seeding
Bottom: *Santalum acuminatum* (quandong) fruit

Top: Lerp scale on leaves of *Eucalyptus camaldulensis* (river red gum)
Bottom: Bloodwood (*Eucalyptus opaca*) gall

Top: Digging for bush potatoes
Centre: *Ipomoea costata* vine (bush potato)
Bottom: *Vigna lanceolata* (pencil yam) tubers

Top: *Marsdenia australis* (bush banana)
Centre: Bush banana leaves
Right: *Podaxis pistillaris* (stalked puffball)

DESERT POPLAR
Codonocarpus cotinifolius
Family: Gyrostemonaceae

Alyawarr	*alkemal*
Anmatyerr	*alkemal*
E. Arrernte	*alkemale*
W. Arrernte	*kalwerte-kalwerte*
Kaytetye	*alkemale*
Pintupi	*kalutu, kanturangu, katati*
Pitjantjatjara	*kaluti, kanturangu, katati*
Warlpiri	*karnturangi, ngapurla, warlkamali*

To 9 m high but often smaller, usually with narrow conical shape. **Bark** smooth, bluish or pinkish grey. **Leaves** leathery, greyish-green. Mature plants often produce such a heavy load of seed heads that upper trunk bends over and sometimes breaks off. Often forms thick scrubs when good seasons follow drought or fire. Grows very quickly but lasts only 5–8 years.

Habitat: Found throughout area with spinifex on sandy soils, or sometimes extending into mulga or onto spinifex hills.

Uses: Mature trees often support a high population of edible grubs (beetle larvae) in the lower trunk and roots — small, but so abundant when available that they provide an important part of the traditional Aboriginal diet at such times. Babies are placed on and under leaves to be cooled by evaporating water (Warl.); leaves lining a large hole serve the same purpose for adults lying on them.

Ref: *Bushfires & Bushtucker* p. 150

NATIVE PEAR
Cynanchum floribundum
Family: Asclepiadaceae

Alyawarr	*angelth, antya*
Anmatyerr	*angelth*
E. Arrernte	*angelthe*
W. Arrernte	*ngelthe*
Kaytetye	*antye*
Warlpiri	*nyarrpurta, yulawari*

Small, multi-stemmed shrub up to 1 m. Twining **branches** and milky **sap**. **Flowers** white. **Fruit** green, drying to a pale yellow. Fruit produced three weeks or more after rain.

Habitat: Usually found in or near sandy watercourses; also on dunes in south. Now fairly rare in Central Australia except in areas free of rabbits, cattle and foreign grasses; was probably more common before they came.

Uses: Young pods are generally eaten raw; older pods and leaves are often steamed. In other areas of Australia the bark of the native pear is an important source of fibre.

Ref: *Bushfires & Bushtucker* p. 157

HOP BUSH
Dodonaea viscosa ssp. *mucronata*
Family: Sapindaceae

Alyawarr	*artart*
W. Arrernte	*irlpe-marnte, tyware*
Pintupi	*nyalpilinyi, walukara*
Pitjantjatjara	*arnginyi, tjininypa, wituluru*
Warlpiri	*jilingu, yanyirlingu*

Glabrous shrub to 2 m. **Leaves** sticky, flat, club shaped. **Flowers** insignificant. **Fruits** distinctive: rounded in side view but strongly three-winged, pink to red in colour, about 1.5 cm in diameter. (A similar species usually given same name by Aboriginal people is described below.)

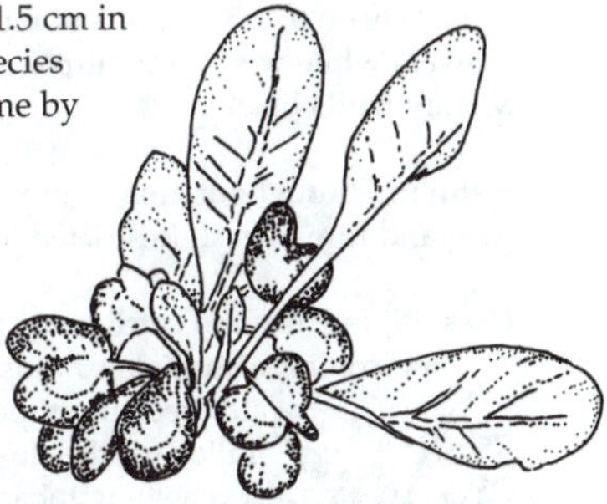

Habitat: Occurs on larger hills throughout the area.

Uses: Medicinal use (Pit. only). Branches are laid in a warm ashpit; patients lie on them and the fumes relieve internal pains.

Dodonaea viscosa ssp. *angustissima*
Similar to *D.* ssp. *mucronata*, but the leaves are narrow with almost parallel sides and are not sticky. Occurs more or less throughout the area, usually on sand dunes. Dead branches retain their leaves and are often used to build shelters.

Ref: *Bushfires & Bushtucker* p. 161

PITURI BUSH, EMU POISON BUSH
Duboisia hopwoodii
Family: Solanaceae

Alyawarr	*petyerr* (?)
E. Anmatyerr	*arekerr* (?)
W. Arrernte	*murnenge*
Kaytetye	*arekerre*
Pintupi	*kungkungu, tjila*
Pitjantjatjara	*kungkungu, kurumaru, tjila, walkalpa*
Warlpiri	*warlkalpa, kirliyi*

Clonal shrub to 2.5 m, often branching from base. **Flowers** white with faint purple streaks inside tube. Mature **fruits** black.

Habitat: Throughout area — most common in south-west and rare in east. Restricted to sandy spinifex areas.

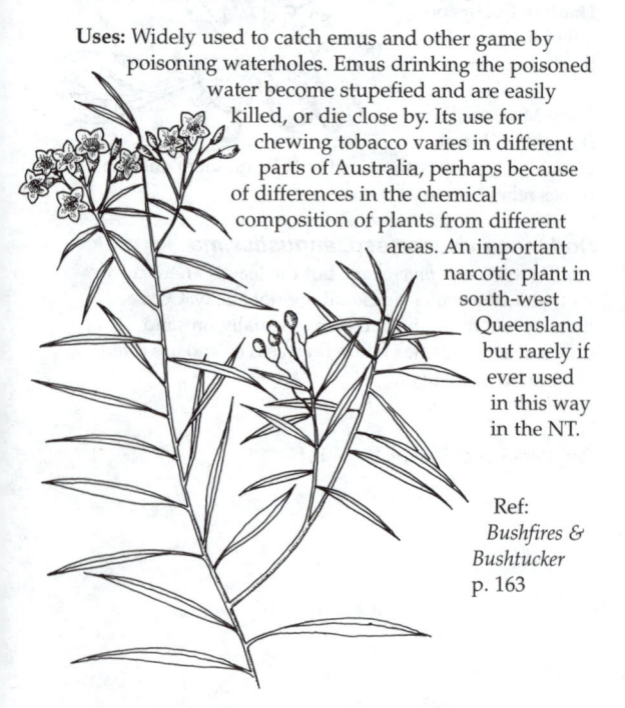

Uses: Widely used to catch emus and other game by poisoning waterholes. Emus drinking the poisoned water become stupefied and are easily killed, or die close by. Its use for chewing tobacco varies in different parts of Australia, perhaps because of differences in the chemical composition of plants from different areas. An important narcotic plant in south-west Queensland but rarely if ever used in this way in the NT.

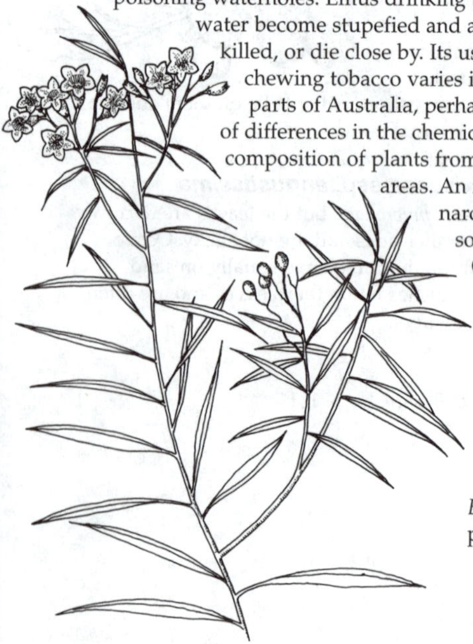

Ref: *Bushfires & Bushtucker* p. 163

RED POVERTY BUSH
Eremophila duttonii
Family: Myoporaceae

Alyawarr	*akwenthey*
Anmatyerr	*akwenthey*
E. Arrernte	*aherre-intenhe*
Kaytetye	*aketntheye*
Pintupi	*multinpa*
Pitjantjatjara	*muntju<u>n</u>pa, munyu<u>n</u>pa*
Warlpiri	*yakunjiyi*

Sticky shrub to 2.5 m. **Leaves** narrow, bright green, clustered at ends of branches. After red **flowers** fall, pink pointed **bracts** enlarge: sometimes mistaken for flowers.

Habitat: Woodlands, usually on gravelly flats; also sometimes in sand, near dunes.

Uses: Pitjantjatjara, Anmatyerr and Alyawarr people consider it to have medicinal properties.

Ref: *Bushfires & Bushtucker* p. 172

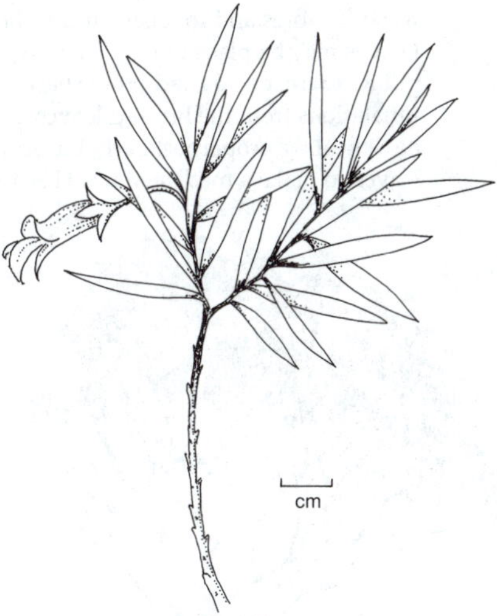

HILL FUCHSIA
Eremophila freelingii
Family: Myoporaceae

Alyawarr	*arreth*
Anmatyerr	*arreth*
Arrernte	*arrethe*
Kaytetye	*arrethe*
Pitjantjatjara	*aratja*
Warlpiri	*miinypa, miyinypa*

Aromatic shrub about 1.5 m high. **Bark** dark. **Leaves** crowded, bluish or grey-green, soft, sticky. **Flowers** lilac.

Habitat: Usually restricted to gravelly hillslopes.

Uses: An important medicinal plant throughout the area. A decoction of the leaves may be drunk or used as a wash for sores and to relieve headaches and chest pains. Leaves may be placed in the nasal septum or used as a pillow to treat colds and other chest complaints. Inhalations from the bruised leaves are considered to have healing properties. Early European settlers used the leaves to make a medicinal tea. Has attractive flowers which are sometimes placed in headbands for decoration during ceremonies.

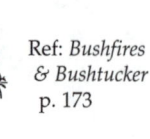

Ref: *Bushfires & Bushtucker* p. 173

EMU BUSH
Eremophila longifolia
Family: Myoporaceae

Alyawarr	*arlarterr, itnwerreng*
E. Anmatyerr	*itnwerreng, utnerreng, unerreng*
W. Anmatyerr	*lhwekelhwek*
E. Arrernte	*utnerrenge*
W. Arrernte	*tnwerrenge, ulpente*
Kaytetye	*wetyenye*
Pintupi	*nga<u>l</u>urrpu*
Pitjantjatjara	*tulypurpa*
Warlpiri	*lukulyuku, ngarlurrpu, winarnkuru, wirnarnkuru*

Large clonal shrub 2–4 m high. **Leaves** soft, dull green, drooping. **Flowers** dull red outside, pink inside. **Fruit** has thin, fleshy, purple covering.

Habitat: Most habitats, though never very abundant.

Uses: Considerable ritual significance for most Central Australian peoples; the leaves, branches and smoke from the leaves are used extensively in ceremonies. Has important medicinal properties, some common to all Central Australian Aboriginal people, others specific to one group. Branches are often used to surround emu flesh in the cooking process. Fruit is not eaten, but is a favoured food of emus. A caterpillar *tnwerrengatye* (W. Arr.), *tnwerrengayt* (Aly'rr) feeds on the leaves of this plant and is an important food source.

Ref: *Bushfires & Bushtucker* p. 176

BIRD-FLOWER GREVILLEA
Grevillea eriostachya
Family: Proteaceae

Pintupi	ka_liny-ka_linypa
Pitjantjatjara	*kaliny-kalinypa, tjuratja* (nectar [?])
Warlpiri	*tipa*

Similar to honey grevillea (*G. juncifolia*) but lower, more spreading; crowded yellow **flowers** grow only on very ends of branches. Flowers produced after rain except during coldest winter months.

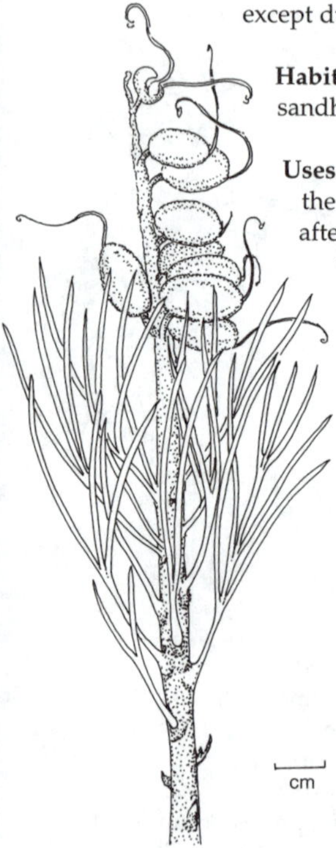

Habitat: Spinifex sandplains and sandhills.

Uses: Abundant honey is found in the flowers and is much sought after. Honey is either sucked from the flowers, or they are steeped in water and the liquid is drunk.

Ref: *Bushfires & Bushtucker* p. 200

HONEY GREVILLEA
Grevillea juncifolia
Family: Proteaceae

Alyawarr	*tharrkarr*
E. Anmatyerr	*tharrkarr*
W. Anmatyerr	*rrwerleng*
E. Arrernte	*irrwerlenge, tyewerrke*
W. Arrernte	*irrwerlenge*
Kaytetye	*tharrkarre*
Pintupi	*ultukunpa, yultukunpa*
Pitjantjatjara	*ultukunpa, ultukunyilypa, yultukunpa, tjuratja* (nectar)
Warlpiri	*walunarri, wirrpinyaru, wiyinyari, yurltukunpa*

Erect shrub to 3.5 m. **Leaves** rigid and sticky. **Flowers** golden-yellow or orange. Flowers produced after rain except during coldest winter months.

Habitat: Mainly in sandy spinifex areas but sometimes also found on hilltops.

Uses: An important plant throughout the area because of the honey found in the flowers: it is either sucked from the flowers, or the flowers are steeped in water to make a sweet drink. E. Warlpiri are reputed to apply bark ash as a healing agent to sores, wounds and other skin conditions.

Ref: *Bushfires & Bushtucker* p. 201

SANDHILL GREVILLEA, RATTLEPOD GREVILLEA
Grevillea stenobotrya
Family: Proteaceae

Alyawarr	*aywel*
E. Anmatyerr	*aywel*
E. Arrernte	*tharrkarre*
W. Arrernte	*irlpare*
Kaytetye	*aywele*
Pintupi	*ananti, nyintilpa, nyinytjilypa, yananti*
Pitjantjatjara	*ilpara, nyintilpa, yaranpa*
Warlpiri	*juntala, pijurna (?), wirrpinyaru*

To 3 m high. **Bark** smooth, greyish, becoming pink on twigs. **Leaves** long and narrow, green above but silvery-green beneath. **Flowers** thin, white or yellowish bottlebrushes. **Pods** similar to honey grevillea (*G. juncifolia*, p. 133) but smooth, and remain (with large-winged **seeds**) on bush for a long period. Flowers after rain.

Habitat: Sandhills: always in red sands, usually on dune crests.

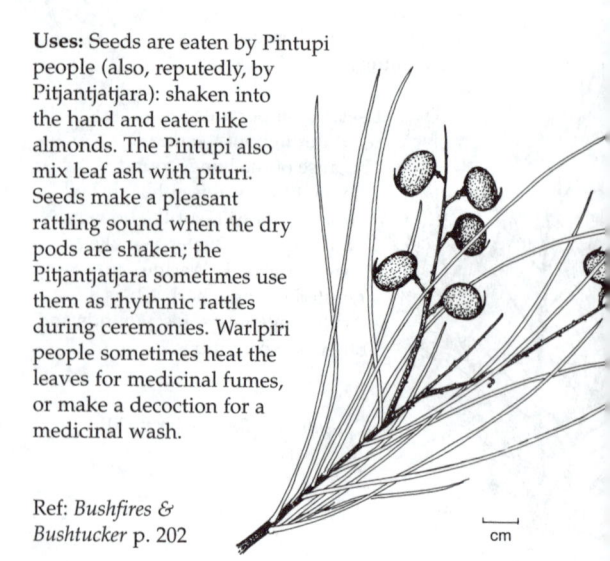

Uses: Seeds are eaten by Pintupi people (also, reputedly, by Pitjantjatjara): shaken into the hand and eaten like almonds. The Pintupi also mix leaf ash with pituri. Seeds make a pleasant rattling sound when the dry pods are shaken; the Pitjantjatjara sometimes use them as rhythmic rattles during ceremonies. Warlpiri people sometimes heat the leaves for medicinal fumes, or make a decoction for a medicinal wash.

Ref: *Bushfires & Bushtucker* p. 202

HOLLY LEAF GREVILLEA
Grevillea wickhamii ssp. *aprica*
Family: Proteaceae

Alyawarr	*kelkareng*
Anmatyerr	*kelkareng*
W. Arrernte	*lyake*
Kaytetye	*kelkarenge*
Pintupi	*yintjilnga*
Pitjantjatjara	*tjilka-tjilkarpa*
Warlpiri	*karlkarangi, lakarrpara, pijalapanpa*

Attractive shrub, about 2.5 m. **Bark** smooth. **Leaves** dull green, holly-like. **Flowers** bright red, loosely arranged. **Fruits** woody.

Habitat: Usually on hillsides, sometimes on sandplains, always with spinifex.

Uses: A clear gum exuding from the branches is often eaten. Holly leaf grevillea has mythologic significance for Alyawarr people.

Ref: *Bushfires & Bushtucker* p. 204

Grevillea species
Family: Proteaceae

Pitjantjatjara *tjarilpa, tjutjur-tjutjurnmalpa, yarailpa*

There is some general uncertainty about the Aboriginal names and uses of the *Grevillea* species. It seems that while holly leaf grevillea and beefwood (p. 176) are given unique names, several other species occuring south of Alice Springs — notably *G. nematophylla* and *G. pterosperma* — and even some *Hakeas* may all be referred to by the same name. Further investigation is required.

Ref: *Bushfires & Bushtucker* p. 204

KURUMARU, SOFT-LEAVED SAND-BUSH
Gyrostemon tepperi and *G. ramulosus*
Family: Gyrostemonaceae

Alyawarr	*irrkwer-irrkwer*
Pintupi	*yawingura*
Pitjantjatjara	*kuru̱maru̱, wilpa-wilpa̱ra*
Warlpiri	*jaka-liirli-jaka-liirli, marrkulya, ngapala-ngapala*

About 1.5 m. **Bark** smooth, pinkish or yellowish. **Foliage** soft. **Leaves** small, narrow, curved; crowded, with green or yellowish-green colour. **Flowers** inconspicuous, pale yellow; male and female flowers occur on different plants. Small rounded **pods** split in half at maturity.
(*G. ramulosus* — *kuru̱maru̱, u̱ntalya* [Pit.] — is about 3 m. Yellow or whitish **bark** becomes corky with age. **Leaves** narrow, curved, dark green. **Fruits** similar to those of *Codonocarpus*, p. 117, but smaller.)

Habitat: Western half of area, found on spinifex sandplains but never very common. (*G. ramulosus* restricted to sand dune crests.)

Uses: W. Pintupi and N. Anmatyerr peoples sometimes use this plant to poison small waterholes to catch game. (The soft wood of *G. ramulosus* is used to carve certain implements. It is now often used to produce animal carvings for sale to tourists.)

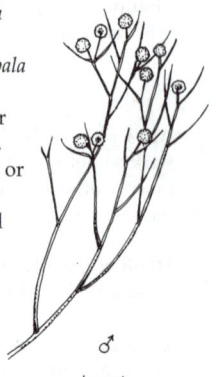

Ref: *Bushfires & Bushtucker* p. 205

G. ramulosus (male)

G. ramulosus (female)

NEEDLE BUSH, NEEDLEWOOD
Hakea leucoptera
Family: Proteaceae

Anmatyerr	*ilpey*
E. Arrernte	*ilpeye*
W. Arrernte	*ilpengke*
Kaytetye	*elpeye*
Pintupi	*mara-wakalpa*
Pitjantjatjara	*mara-wakalpa*, *piri-piri* (= fingernail, claw), *upi*
Warlpiri	*mara-wakalpa*

Clonal shrub or small tree, about 3 m. **Leaves** needle-like, about 6 cm long. **Flowers** white or yellow, occur in small clusters. **Fruits** woody.

Habitat: Widespread, but usually in semi-saline soils.

Uses: Water may be obtained from the roots, but they are probably only used this way in the driest areas. Branches retain their leaves when dry and make good shelters.

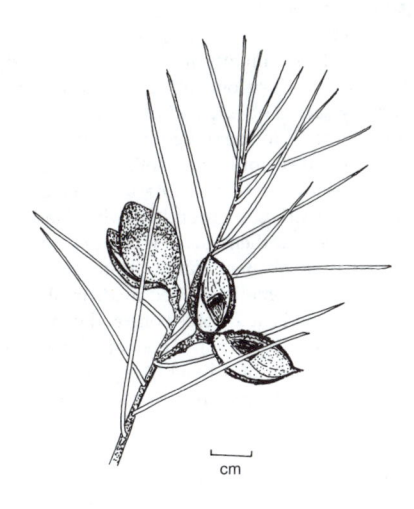

Ref: *Bushfires & Bushtucker* p. 209

TEATREE, PAPERBARK
Melaleuca glomerata
Family: Myrtaceae

Alyawarr	*thankw, perety*
Anmatyerr	*irlperl, ilperl*
Arrernte	*irlperle watentye*
Kaytetye	*peretye*
Pintupi	*ilypili, palyku, tjantutu, yilypili*
Pitjantjatjara	*ilpili, mintipi (?), piyalpa*
Warlpiri	*kintilarri, kupangardi, pakarli*

About 3 m high. **Bark** white, papery. **Leaves** narrow, grey-green. **Flowers** yellow or creamy, producing small **capsules** which cluster around stem.

Habitat: Around salt lakes and claypans or in small watercourses in hills.

Uses: The papery bark of this shrub (and other species described below) is used extensively: commonly, to make sheaths for stone knives and wallets for carrying sacred objects and other materials. Large slabs are often used for carrying pituri and other trade items, also as blankets for babies, splints for broken bones or bandages for wounds. The bark is used as a brush, for dabbing blood onto ground paintings and so on. Branches retain their leaves when dry, and are often used to build shelters. Fumes from smouldering branches are sometimes used medicinally (Pit.). Branches can be laid across one end of a narrow pool and then pushed through the water by a group of people as a kind of fish net (Arr.). Wood is sometimes used for certain implements or for children's spears.

Ref: *Bushfires & Bushtucker* p. 226

SANDHILL TEATREE AND OTHER TEATREES
Melaleuca lasiandra, *Melaleuca* species
Family: Myrtaceae

About 2.5 m. **Bark** fine, papery. **Leaves** silvery, grey-green. Creamy yellow **flowers** occur in loose spikes.

Habitat: Usually at base of sand dunes; also near salt lakes and claypans.

Uses: See teatree (*M. glomerata*) previous page.

Other species, mostly restricted to the larger ranges, include *M. bracteata*, *M. dissitiflora*, and *M. trichostachya*. Generally given the same names as the preceding species and used in same way. *M. fulgens* ssp. *corrugata*, a rare species apparently restricted to the summits of the Musgrave and Petermann ranges, is a highly aromatic plant and may be used in some way.

Ref: *Bushfires & Bushtucker* p. 227

Melaleuca lasiandra

BUTTERFLY BUSH
Petalostylis cassioides
Family: Caesalpiniaceae

Alyawarr	*intyern*
E. Anmatyerr	*intyern*
Kaytetye	*ntyerne*
Pitjantjatjara	*kuyu-turu-turu*
Warlpiri	*jakanypa, karrkarnpa*

About 1.5 m high. **Bark** brownish-pink. **Leaves** somewhat fern-like. **Flower** attractive; composed of five large orange petals. **Pods** forcibly eject seeds when mature.

Habitat: Spinifex sandplains and sandhills, in red sands or on gravelly soils. Less common in south-eastern third of area.

Uses: A sweet exudation from this plant is eaten. E. Warlpiri use the leaves for medicinal purposes: heated, crushed and rubbed on the skin for various ailments.

Ref: *Bushfires & Bushtucker* p. 243

MINT BUSH
Prostanthera striatiflora
Family: Lamiaceae

Alyawarr	*apmwer*
E. Anmatyerr	*apmwer, amwer*
E. Arrernte	*atnurlke, arrwatnurlke*
W. Arrernte	*arretnurlke*
Kaytetye	*arntep-arntepe* (?)
Pitjantjatjara	*mintjingka, karinga̱na*
Warlpiri	*warlkalpa*

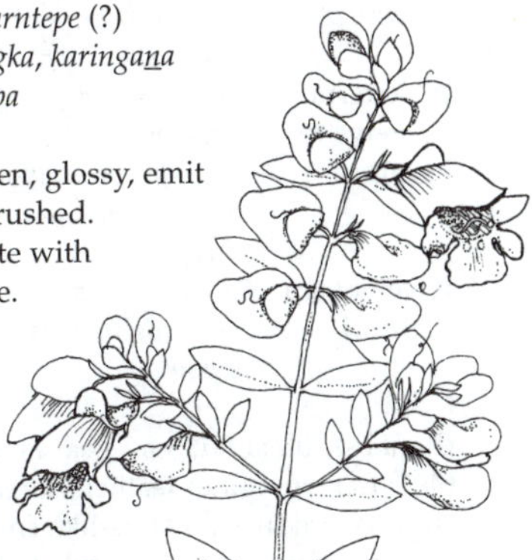

1–2 m high. **Leaves** green, glossy, emit pleasant odour when crushed. **Flowers** attractive; white with purple striations in tube.

Habitat: Mostly on hills with crystalline rocks, in central and south-western half of area.

Uses: Considered a useful medicinal plant. Pounded leaves are mixed with fat and used as an ointment, or a decoction is used as a medicinal wash. The Warlpiri are said to use crushed leaves as emu poison in the same way as the pituri bush (*Duboisia*, p. 128).

Ref: *Bushfires & Bushtucker* p. 252

PLUM BUSH, WILD PLUM
Santalum lanceolatum
Family: Santalaceae

Alyawarr	*alkwa*
Anmatyerr	*alkwa, ankwerley* (E. Anm.), *ankwerlay* (W. Anm.)
E. Arrernte	*alkwe, ankweleye, arrankweye*
W. Arrernte	*rrankweye*
Kaytetye	*ankweleye*
Pintupi	*arrnguli, kanturangu, kupata, nyunnguli, yarrnguli*
Pitjantjatjara	*arnguli, kupata*
Warlpiri	*marrkirdi, mukaki, yankurlayi*

Clonal shrub about 3 m. **Leaves** drooping, bluish-green, rather leathery. Creamy white **flowers** produce an olive-like **fruit** which matures from green to purple to black. Fruits produced after rain at any time of year except for two coldest months.

Habitat: Throughout the area in most habitats. Can be quite common in certain areas, but heavy grazing by cattle and rabbits has reduced overall abundance.

Uses: Fruit has a pleasant, rather bland taste, but the proportion of edible flesh is low: an important food but not a staple. Dried fruits, collected from under the bush, are easily reconstituted in water. Warlpiri people are said to remove the shells from roasted seeds and grind the kernels into edible paste. Red juice squeezed from the fruit is sometimes used as a dye. Paste from ground kernels is used as a medicinal liniment (Pit.).

Ref: *Bushfires & Bushtucker* p. 261

CAUSTIC VINE
Sarcostemma viminale
ssp. *australe*
Family: Asclepiadaceae

POISONOUS

SHRUB

Alyawarr	*amikwel, mamarlety*
Anmatyerr	*kwep-kwep*
E. Arrernte	*kwele-kwele*
W. Arrernte	*ipatye-ipatye*
Kaytetye	*kwepe-kwepe*
Pitjantjatjara	*kungka-kungka, ipi-ipi*
Warlpiri	*kiji-kiji, kupu-kupu, ngapurlu-ngapurlu*

Dense shrubby plant. **Branches** leafless, tangled and twining. **Flowers** pale green. **Pods** contain numerous feathery **seeds**. When injured, plant exudes copious milky sap. *Highly poisonous.*

Habitat: Usually found on rocky hills; sometimes in mulga or gidgee scrubs.

Uses: Sap is used to cure persistent skin and eye complaints: by smoke treatment (Pit.) or by placing sick babies on compressed branches (Warl.). W. Arrernte people regard this plant as a feminine symbol; milk-like sap is dabbed on women's breasts during ritual proceedings. (The literal translation of most Aboriginal names for this plant is 'milk-milk'.) The white latex is applied medicinally for various external complaints by Aboriginal people across a wide area of Australia.

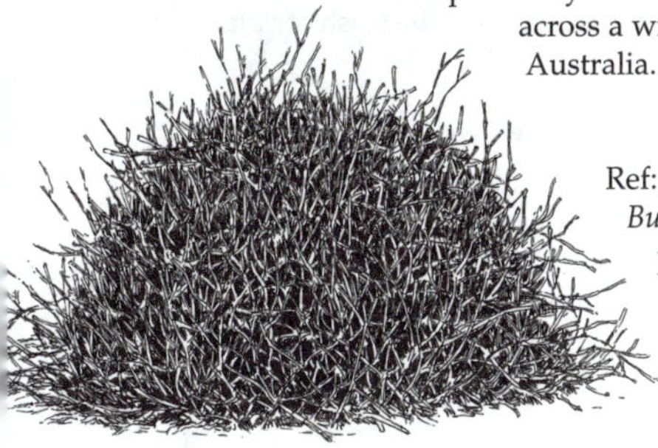

Ref: *Bushfires & Bushtucker* p. 262

CASSIAS
Senna artemisioides subspecies
Family: Caesalpiniaceae

Alyawarr	*apwen, arey-arey, areyawarr*
E. Anmatyerr	*apwen, areyawarr, manatwerrp*
W. Anmatyerr	*apwen, manatwerrp, ngkwert, kwert-kwert*
E. Arrernte	*apwene, ingkwerte*
Kaytetye	*apwene, pwerethe, manatwerrpe, kwarratetherre*
Pintupi	*punti*
Pitjantjatjara	*arapita, inuntji* (= fresh plant growth, blossoms), *pilani, punti, untunu*
Warlpiri	*marnturlpu, pijuna, purnti, wariyi, yiriwurrunyu*

There are ten different subspecies of *Senna artemisioides* in Central Australia; classification is difficult as hybridisation between species appears to be quite common. The two species described are fairly easily recognised and generally given discrete Aboriginal names. Aboriginal people recognise differences between the other common species, but use only one name. Sometimes different forms are referred to as 'male' and 'female', or sibling plants.

These plants are all woody shrubs greater than 0.5 m tall with similar yellow flowers. **Pods** are distinctive, being broad and papery.

Edible grubs are found in the roots; flowers are employed in ritual decoration. Leaves of ssp. *helmsii* and ssp. *oligophylla* are used to smoke babies (Warl.). Twigs of ssp. *helmsii* are burnt to produce ash for pituri (Warl.).

Ref: *Bushfires & Bushtucker* p. 264

BROOM BUSH, DESERT CASSIA
Senna artemisioides ssp. *artemisioides* and *filifolia*
Family: Caesalpiniaceae

Alyawarr	*apwen* (S. a. filifolia)
Anmatyerr	*apwen* (S. a. filifolia)
E. Arrernte	*apwene* (S. a. filifolia)
Kaytetye	*pwene, pwerethe* (S. a. filifolia)

About 2 m high. **Leaflets** soft, narrow. **Flowers** attractive bright yellow. **Pods** flat, papery. Ssp. *filifolia* has only one or two pairs of bright green leaflets; ssp. *artemisioides* has 3–10 pairs of dull green leaflets. Quick growing and relatively short lived.

Habitat: Most habitats, but commonest in interzonal areas.

Uses: Edible grubs are extracted from the roots of mature or dead plants. Seeds may sometimes be eaten, after treatment, in some southern areas (further investigation is required). Leaves of ssp. *artemisioides* are boiled (E. Warl.); the resultant red liquid is applied as a medicinal wash to ease pain. Leaves of ssp. *filifolia* are used to smoke babies. Flowers and leaves are commonly used for decoration during ceremonies; twigs are often used in the construction of elaborate head-dresses. Wood is sometimes used for spear barbs. Foliage has many uses including material for shelters, fly swats, mats for meat and other foods, and making simple dolls for children.

S. a. filifolia

Ref: *Bushfires & Bushtucker* p. 265

CHOCOLATE BUSH, FIREBUSH
Senna pleurocarpa
Family: Caesalpiniaceae

Alyawarr	*ilenyenp*
E. Anmatyerr	*ilenyenp, iylenyenp*
E. Arrernte	*lyenyenpe*
W. Arrernte	*lirlarre*
Kaytetye	*eylenyenpe*
Pintupi	*kalpirr-kalpirrpa*
Pitjantjatjara	*karpil-karpilpa*
Warlpiri	*karlpirr-karlpirrpa, kulinkilinpa, pitarl-pitarlpa*

Clonal sub-shrub about 0.5 m. **Flowers** attractive, yellow. **Pods** have distinct raised line down centre. **Seeds** black, wrinkled.

Habitat: Common in red sand with spinifex.

Uses: Grubs found in the roots are widely eaten. Flowers and foliage are used for ritual decoration.

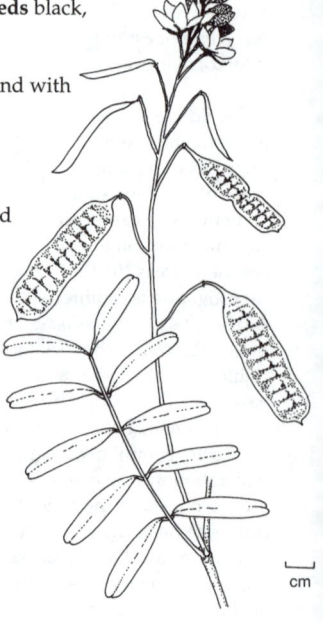

Ref: *Bushfires & Bushtucker* p. 266

DESERT THRYPTOMENE
Thryptomene maisonneuvii
Family: Myrtaceae

SHRUB

Pitjantjatjara   *pukara, waputi*

About 70 cm high. **Bark** pink. **Leaves** very small, dark green. **Flowers** white or pink with red centres; can be very prolific.

Habitat: Mostly south of latitude 23°, at the base of sand dunes.

Uses: Pitjantjatjara people collect dew from these plants when they are in flower in the cooler months. The liquid obtained is sweetened by honey from the flowers, providing both food and water.

Ref: *Bushfires & Bushtucker* p. 285

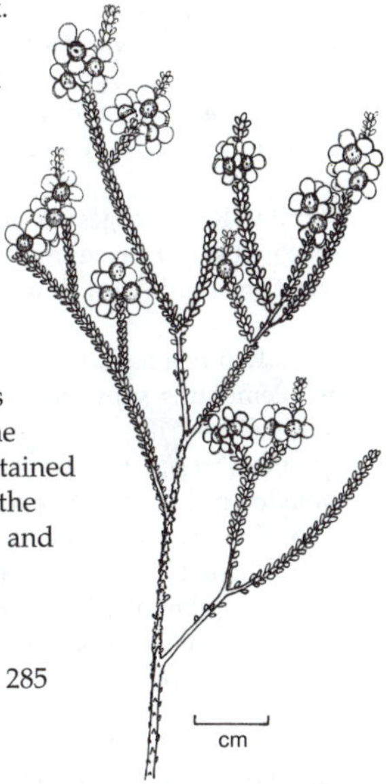

GRASS TREE, BLACK BOY
Xanthorrhea thorntonii
Family: Liliaceae

W. Arrernte	*lunkere*
Pitjantjatjara	*kata-kultu, kata-puru, ulpa, urara*
Warlpiri	*yurlurnkuru*

Typical grass tree, about 2 m. **Flowers** borne on thick stalks a further 2 m high.

Habitat: Rare. Largest populations found west and south-west of Hermannsburg; occasional scattered stands in south-west third of area.

Uses: Reddish resin found oozing from the trunk is used as a cementing substance. Contrary to reports from some writers, it is considered inferior to resin from spinifex (*Triodia*, p. 24 ff.) or even desert mulga (*Acacia minyura*, p. 101). Its main value lies in the ease of collection. Although other gums and resins are strengthened by adding plant fibre, in Central Australia this one apparently is not. White basal parts of the inner leaves are said to be eaten (unconfirmed).

Ref: *Bushfires & Bushtucker*
p. 298

TREES

MULGA
Acacia aneura
Family: Mimosaceae

Alyawarr	*artety*
Anmatyerr	*artety*
E. Arrernte	*artetye*
W. Arrernte	*irtetye*
Kaytetye	*artetye*
Pintupi	*kurrku, mantja, manytja, wanari*
Pitjantjatjara	*kalpilya, minyura, nguyuruma* (fungus), *puyukara, tjamalya, wanari, kurku* (lerp sap [?])
Warlpiri	*manja, wanajirti, wardiji, yurnanji* (mulga scrub), *yuwurrku* (mulga scrub)

5–12 m tree/shrub with very variable forms. **Bark** rough. **Leaves** vary from short and broad to long, almost cylindrical. **Flower spikes** cylindrical. **Pods** flat. **Seeds** medium-sized, oval, hard coat. Blue mulga (more fire tolerant) has distinctive bluish-green leaves. *A. paraneura* has very long, drooping leaves. Can flower at any time of year following heavy rain, but needs subsequent rain to produce seeds.

Habitat: Widespread, occurs in dense stands (mulga scrubs) usually on flat red-earth plains, but also on hillsides or between dunes. Scattered trees grow in a wide variety of habitats.

Uses: Seeds are an important food: this is the most common tree in Central Australia, with always a few trees bearing pods for several months even in dry years. Seeds can be collected from the tree or the ground, cleaned, roasted and ground to a paste similar to peanut butter and at least as nutritious. Mulga wood is relatively easy to work when green, dries hard and strong and rarely splits, so is the most important source of wood for implements. Wood from the trunk makes shields, boomerangs, woomeras, digging sticks, fighting spears, adzes, fighting clubs and sacred objects. Dead trees are important for firewood: decaying mulga splits readily, and only the larger dead trees cannot be uprooted. Ash from twigs is often used for pituri. Leaves are used as a mat for food and sacred objects, to form platforms in tree forks for storage, or as a broom to clear the ground.

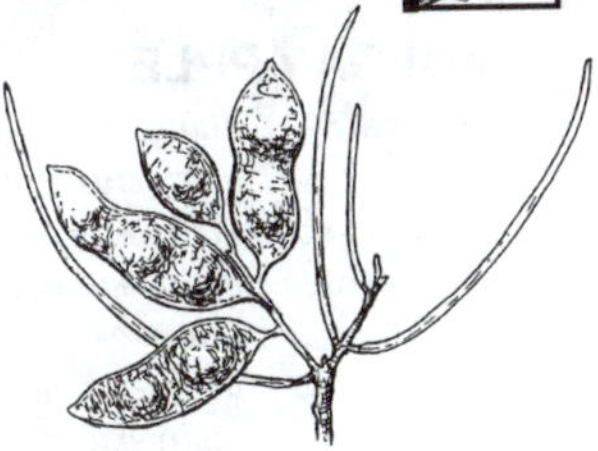

Ref: *Bushfires & Bushtucker* p. 88

MULGA: ASSOCIATED FOODS
LERP SCALE

Alyawarr	*arlperl, arlperlamp*
Anmatyerr	*arlperl*
E. Arrernte	*arlperle*
W. Arrernte	*thengarlpe*
Kaytetye	*arlperlampe*
Pintupi	*tjamanpa, urranpa, yurranpa*
Pitjantjatjara	*yuranpa, mirngalypa, mangirpa, kurkunytjungu, kurku* (sap)
Warlpiri	*yalypilyi*

Lerp *Austrotachardia acaciae* often infests large areas of mulga. Numerous small red protruberances on terminal branches exude large quantities of honey(dew), an extremely popular food treat. Branches are broken off and the honey is sucked up by drawing twigs through the mouth; alternatively, branches are taken back to camp and soaked in water to produce a sweet drink.

MULGA APPLE

Alyawarr	*ataltyakwerl, artetyetyakwerl*
Anmatyerr	*ataltyakwerl*
E. Arrernte	*ataltyakwerle, taltyekwerle*
W. Arrernte	*ataltyekwerle*
Kaytetye	*ataltyakwerle*
Pintupi	*karrulykurra, takuṯurru, tarruḻka, tarrunpa*
Pitjantjatjara	*tarulka, tjarulka*
Warlpiri	*larrunka, rdarrunka, tanjakurlu*

Marble-shaped wasp gall with small protruberances scattered over it. The small white grub in the centre is considered the sweetest part. Other more common galls are not edible.

Ref: *Bushfires & Bushtucker* p. 90

MYALL GIDGEE, NORTHERN MYALL
Acacia calcicola
Family: Mimosaceae

W. Arrernte   *irrakwetye*
Pitjantjatjara   *ikaṯuka*

Shrubby tree, 4 m. **Bark** dark, rough. **Leaves** bluish-green.

Habitat: Limestone, sand-covered limestone. Mostly occurs south of Alice Springs with small scattered populations north of the Macdonnell Ranges.

Uses: Wood is hard, used for artefacts, and favoured as firewood. Leaf ash is used with pituri.

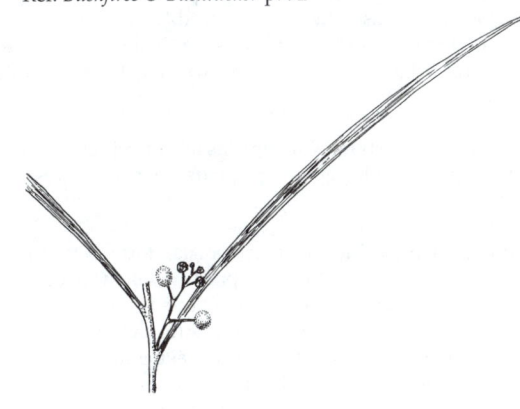

Ref: *Bushfires & Bushtucker* p. 92

DOGWOOD
Acacia coriacea ssp. *seriocophylla*
Family: Mimosaceae

Alyawarr	*awenth, ntyerrm* (seeds)
E. Anmatyerr	*awenth, ntyerrm* (seeds)
W. Anmatyerr	*akerlperr, ntyerrm* (seeds), *ntyerrp* (seeds)
E. Arrernte	*awenthe*
W. Arrernte	*pangkwene*
Kaytetye	*awetnthe, ntyerrme* (seeds)
Pintupi	*kunapuka*; seedpod: *irrkili, pangkuna, yirrkili*
Pitjantjatjara	*kunapuka, mulupuka*
Warlpiri	*kunarnturu, pangkuna, wakirlpirri*; seeds: *pirlarla, rdili, yinjirrpi*; drink from seeds: *nungkarli*

Small shrubby tree 3–6 m. **Bark** pale, corky. **Leaves** long, greyish-green. **Flowers** pale yellow. **Pods** long, twisted, constricted between seeds; when green, difficult to make out against leaves. **Seeds** large, black with large bright orange aril; hard coated. Drought tolerant.

Habitat: Mostly spinifex sandplains (also sandhills); usually grows with feather-top spinifex, north and west of Alice Springs.

Uses: Regular production of seeds makes this an important food plant. When the pods are fully formed but still green, large numbers are collected and lightly roasted, usually on a burning spinifex tussock. This dries up the bitter juices in the pod, making them easy to open and giving the seeds a pleasant smoked flavour. Hardened seeds are collected from pods or picked up off the ground, soaked until the arils are swollen and then mashed by hand with water to form a kind of milk, which is drunk. Timber is favoured for boomerangs and spears. Twig ash is used with pituri, and burnt bark for decoration.

Ref: *Bushfires & Bushtucker* p. 93

IRONWOOD
Acacia estrophiolata
Family: Mimosaceae

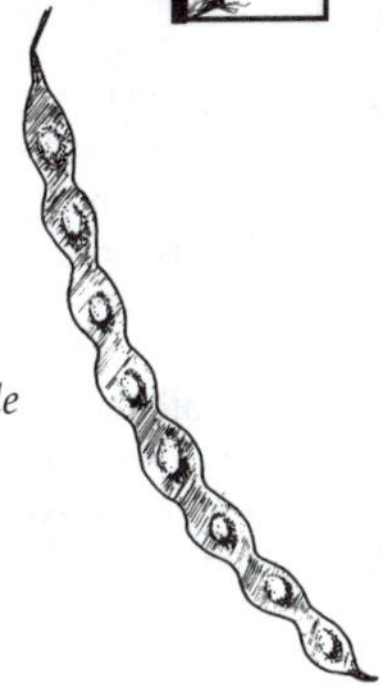

Alyawarr	*atheng, athimp*
E. Anmatyerr	*athimp, athengarlperl* (gum)
W. Anmatyerr	*atheng, atyarnp, tyarnpangkwarl* (gum)
E. Arrernte	*athenge, atyarnpe*
W. Arrernte	*tywarnpe*
Kaytetye	*atheympe, atheympe ngkwarle* (gum)
Pintupi	*walakarri*
Pitjantjatjara	*tjau, utjanypa*
Warlpiri	*yajarnpi, wajarnpi, walirri*

Graceful tree 12–15 m. **Leaves** narrow, dense, pendulous, giving willow-like appearance. Juvenile plants: wider, shorter, spiny leaves — quite different in appearance. (In harsher spinifex country juvenile foliage is often never lost.) **Seeds** medium-sized, hard.

Habitat: Scattered trees in woodland communities.

Uses: Seeds are eaten in the southern part of the area. Medicinal wash is made from the root bark. The trunk exudes prized sweet white gum and red or black medicinal gum. Wood is favoured as firewood and for artefacts. Bark ash is used with pituri. Ironwood is a source for lerp honeydew.

Ref: *Bushfires & Bushtucker* p. 97

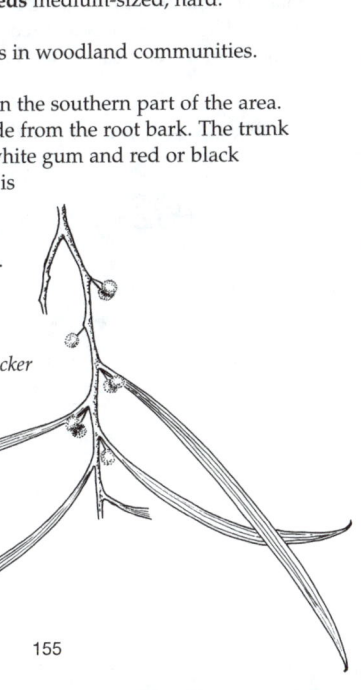

GEORGINA GIDGEE
Acacia georginae
Family: Mimosaceae

Alyawarr	*irrwenyenk, rrwenyenk, tnwanth*
E. Anmatyerr	*urrenyenk, kikarre* (resin)
W. Anmatyerr	*rrwenyenk*
E. Arrernte	*urrenyenke, utnanthe*
Kaytetye	*errwenyenke*; resin: *teykarre, keykarre*

Small, usually gnarled-looking tree about 5 m. **Leaves** grey, with noxious odour when crushed. **Bark** dark, rough. **Flowers** globular, also malodorous. **Pods** broad, flat, twisted. *Seeds can be very poisonous; avoid at all costs.*

Habitat: Many communities. Can often form extensive scrubs, more or less east of the Stuart Highway.

Uses: Edible grubs are found in the roots; edible resin is obtained from the trunk. Good for firewood — it burns slow and hot — and shade. Excellent for windbreaks. Wood from the branches is used for boomerangs.

Ref: *Bushfires & Bushtucker* p. 100

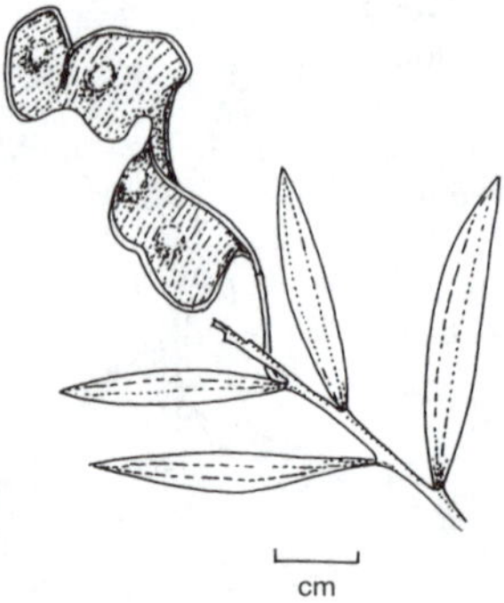

HILL MULGA
Acacia macdonnelliensis
Family: Mimosaceae

Alyawarr	*irrar* (?)
E. Anmatyerr	*arleth-arleth*
W. Arrernte	*irrkwarteke*
Kaytetye	*arleth-arlethe*

Small tree similar to mulga but usually shrubbier-looking. **Bark** darker, more deeply fissured. **Pods** narrow.

Habitat: Common on sandstone and some quartzite hills.

Uses: Seeds are eaten (Aly'rr). Good for firewood. Timber is used for artefacts, especially heavy fighting spears.

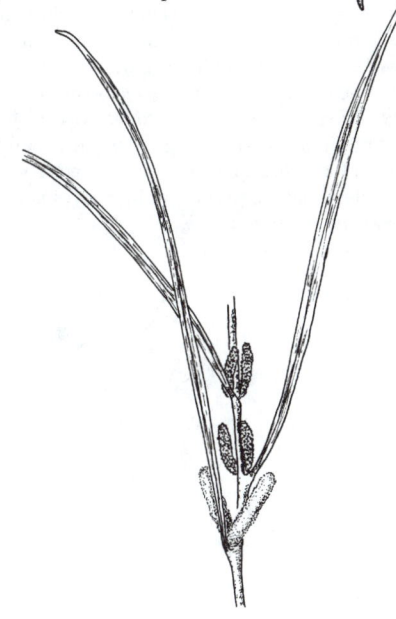

Ref: *Bushfires & Bushtucker* p. 107

BLACK GIDGEE
Acacia pruinocarpa
Family: Mimosaceae

Anmatyerr	*arntepal*
W. Arrernte	*tawe*
Kaytetye	*marntapale*
Pintupi	*mantala, tjawu* (= edible gum in general)
Pitjantjatjara	*itawara, mulyurpa, nyurilypi, tjau* (= edible gum in general)
Warlpiri	*marntarla, marntapali*

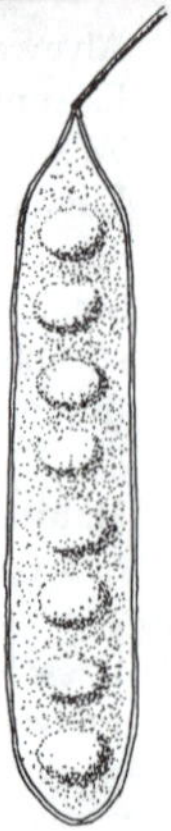

Large, multi-stemmed, often spreading tree to 5 m. **Bark** smooth, grey. **Leaves** flat, stiff, dull bluish-green. **Flowers** golden yellow, can be spectacular. **Pods** flat. **Seeds** medium-sized, rounded, hard, produced only in summer.

Habitat: Sandplains and scree slopes.

Uses: Seeds are sometimes eaten but are difficult to remove from the pod. Plant is more commonly prized for sweet white or yellowish sap that exudes from the trunk. The flowers, and a lerp scale occasionally found on the leaves and stems, also provide sweets. Roots are used for hunting spears. Twig ash is particularly favoured for pituri. Green bark is chewed to stimulate saliva when making spinifex resin. Leaves may be used for smoking mothers and babies, and seeds are used somehow to relieve headaches.

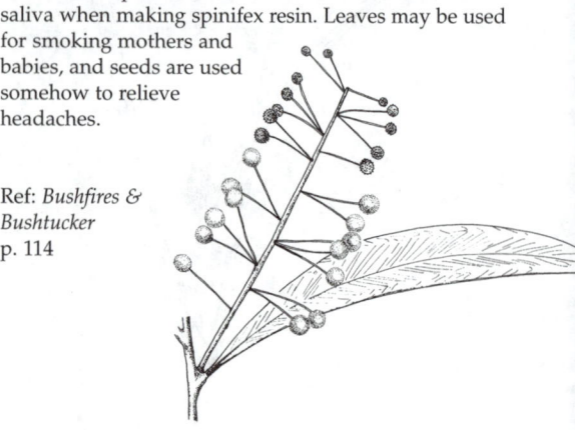

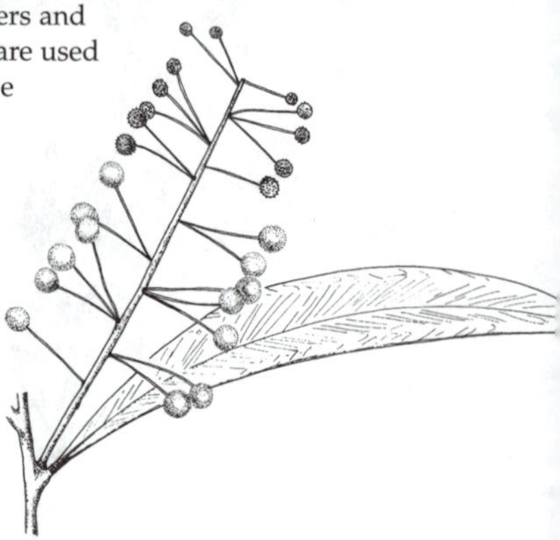

Ref: *Bushfires & Bushtucker* p. 114

DESERT OAK
Allocasuarina decaisneana
Family: Casuarinaceae

E. Anmatyerr	*arrkep*
W. Anmatyerr	*kwerrkar*
E. Arrernte	*irrkepe*
W. Arrernte	*arrkepe*
Kaytetye	*errkepe*
Pintupi	*intarra, kurpa, kurrkapi, kurrkara, nyirrpi, ularrangu, witirrpa, yintarra, yulanti (?), yularrangu, tatu* (seedpod)
Pitjantjatjara	*kurkapi, kurkara, kiritjiti* (sweet sap)
Warlpiri	*kurrkapi, kurrkara*

Large, graceful tree to 10 m. **Bark** dark, scaly, very thick and rough. Drooping **branchlets**. **Foliage** long and needle like. **Fruit** dark heavy cones. Juvenile plants are quite different: straight and erect with short stiff branches growing off single trunk.

Habitat: Spinifex sandplains and sandhills, north to Yuendumu and east to western fringes of Simpson Desert. Often forms large stands in sandy spinifex.

Uses: Cones are lightly roasted to release seed for eating, usually when it is still green. In warm weather, nearly mature cones release a sweet white substance; this is either eaten immediately or cones are soaked in water and the liquid is drunk. Wood is used for clubs and special heavy fighting spears (often traded over great distances). Dead wood is favoured for firewood and also produces ash for pituri.

Ref: *Bushfires & Bushtucker* p. 122

WHITEWOOD
Atalaya hemiglauca
Family: Sapindaceae

Alyawarr	*atnwekert*
E. Anmatyerr	*arlperr, arlperrenhayt* (grub), *arlperrayt* (grub)
W. Anmatyerr	*arlperr, arlperrenh* (grub)
E. Arrernte	*arlperre*
W. Arrernte	*irlperre*
Kaytetye	*arlperre* (tree), *arlperrayte* (grub), *arlperretnhayte* (grub)
Warlpiri	*wanukurdu, yarralyuku*

To 7 m high. **Bark** scaly grey. **Leaves** pale green, leathery. **Flowers** creamy. **Fruit** winged, floats with spiralling motion when falling from tree; can be blown some distance.

Habitat: Found in most non-spinifex communities, but less common in far south, especially south-east.

Uses: Trunk and roots harbour edible witchetty grubs. White sap often exuding from the trunk is also eaten. Soft, white wood is especially favoured for ornaments used in ceremonies. Selected sticks are cut so that shavings, still attached, form small pine-tree-like ornaments. Seeds are often used as toy helicopters by children.

Ref: *Bushfires & Bushtucker* p. 129

DESERT KURRAJONG
Brachychiton gregorii
Family: Sterculiaceae

Alyawarr	*apeng*
Anmatyerr	*apeng, ngkweyang* (seed)
E. Arrernte	*apenge*
W. Arrernte	*ngalte*
Kaytetye	*apenge, ngkweyange* (seed)
Pintupi	*ngalta*
Pitjantjatjara	*ngalta, anpiri* (tap root)
Warlpiri	*ngalta*

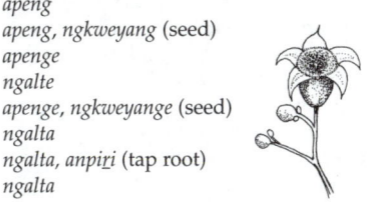

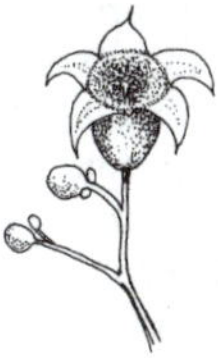

To 8 m high, often multi-trunked. **Bark** smooth. **Leaves** smooth and shiny. **Flowers** pale yellow. **Fruits** woody, containing up to 12 seeds. Outer seed coats papery, more-or-less fused and covered with fine irritant hairs.

Habitat: Spinifex sandplains and sandhills, usually near watercourses or hills. Scattered populations south-west of Alice Springs; isolated populations in east at Angarapa and Ammaroo Station.

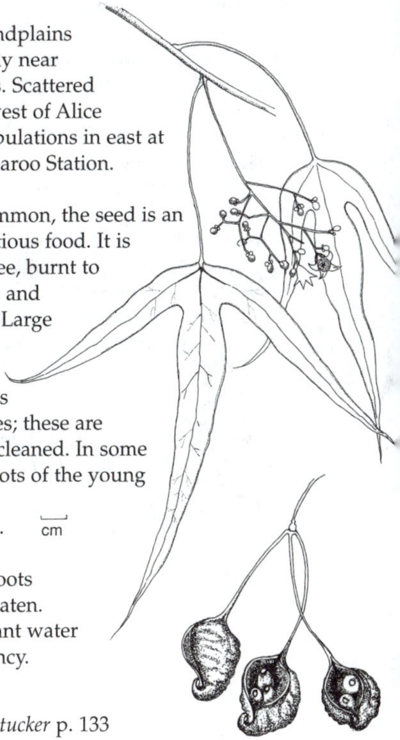

Uses: Where it is common, the seed is an important and nutritious food. It is collected from the tree, burnt to remove irritant hairs and ground into a paste. Large amounts are also deposited by birds in dung or coughings near certain rockholes; these are easily gathered and cleaned. In some areas, the swollen roots of the young plants are roasted, de-barked and eaten. Flowers and large grubs found in the roots are also sometimes eaten. Roots are an important water source in an emergency.

Ref: *Bushfires & Bushtucker* p. 133

NATIVE PINE
Callitris glaucophylla
Family: Cupressaceae

Alyawarr	*apmikw*
E. Anmatyerr	*amikw, apmikw*
W. Anmatyerr	*anngart, rlwek*
E. Arrernte	*irlweke*
W. Arrernte	*alkngarte*
Kaytetye	*apmeykwe*
Pintupi	*mulku*
Pitjantjatjara	*kuli, kulpuru, kulilypuru*
Warlpiri	*wanngardi*

Attractive tree around 6 m. Lower **bark** rough. **Leaves** blue-green, covered with small scales. **Fruit** woody, rounded before they open.

Habitat: All major ranges. Restricted to areas on hills which normally escape fire.

Uses: Medicinal uses (except Pin., Pit.). Leaves and resin are crushed, then either soaked in water for a body wash or mixed with fat and rubbed on the body for various ailments. Twigs are burnt to produce a pleasant odour for babies. The resin, mixed with kangaroo dung for extra strength, is sometimes used as an adhesive (Warl.); wood is sometimes used for implements (Warl.). Dead wood is thought to smell good when burnt, but is rarely used for cooking as it taints food.

Ref: *Bushfires & Bushtucker* p. 135

BEAN TREE, BATS-WING CORAL TREE
Erythrina vespertilio
Family: Fabaceae

Alyawarr	*atywerety*
Anmatyerr	*atywerety, inernt* (seed)
E. Arrernte	*aparrtye, atyweretye, inernte*
Kaytetye	*atyweretye*
Pintupi	*ininti, yininti*
Pitjantjatjara	*ininti*
Warlpiri	*yinirnti*

Tree 8–10 m. **Bark** pale. **Branches** thorny. **Leaves** often fall during winter. **Flowers** attractive, bright red, appear in spring or summer before new leaves. **Seeds** hard, shiny, usually bright red, sometimes yellow.

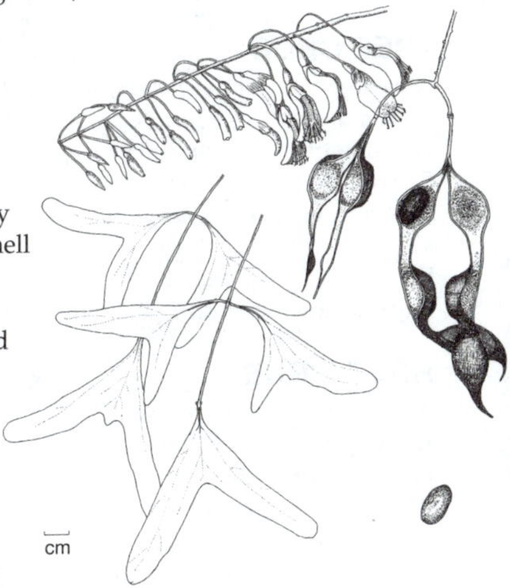

Habitat: Usually associated with watercourses; woodland. Does not grow naturally south of Macdonnell Ranges.

Uses: Warlpiri and Alyawarr people eat the roots of seedling trees — about the size and shape of a large carrot — after roasting and removing the bark. A type of edible grub forming a 'nest' in the tree is also said to be eaten. Wood is very light and easily worked, and is favoured for shields and bowls for carrying babies, water and other materials. Often used as the soft-wood component in the fire-making process. Seeds are used as ornaments, especially necklaces.

Ref: *Bushfires & Bushtucker* p. 179

RIVER RED GUM
Eucalyptus camaldulensis var. *obtusa*
Family: Myrtaceae

TREE

Alyawarr	*aper*
Anmatyerr	*aper*
E. Arrernte	*apere*
W. Arrernte	*pere*
Kaytetye	*aylpele*
Pintupi	*itara, ngapiri, pipalya, yitara*
Pitjantjatjara	*apara, itara, piipalya*
Warlpiri	*ngapiri, kunjumarra*

TREE GRUB

Alyawarr	*apereng-ayerr, aylperlayt, ingweneng*
E. Anmatyerr	*ingweneng*
W. Anmatyerr	*perlanty, ngweneng*
E. Arrernte	*ingwenenge*
W. Arrernte	*ingwenenge, ltheneye*
Kaytetye	*aylpelayte*
Pintupi	*palkapati*
Pitjantjatjara	*ilytjaliti, palkapiti*

ROOT GRUB

Alyawarr	*ahekwenayt*
Anmatyerr	*ahekwenayt*
E. Anmatyerr	*ahekwen*
W. Anmatyerr	*mpaty*
E. Arrernte	*ahernenge*
Pitjantjatjara	*maku unganungu*

HONEY

Alyawarr	*aperarnt, aperengaleng*
E. Anmatyerr	*aperarntw, aperarnt, aperengelengel*
W. Anmatyerr	*mamp*
E. Arrernte	*itethelpe*
Kaytetye	*aperengelengele*
Warlpiri	*jurlarda*

LERP

Alyawarr	*aperelty, peralty*
Anmatyerr	*aperelty, perelty*
E. Arrernte	*aperaltye*
W. Arrernte	*peraltye*
Kaytetye	*peraltye*
Pintupi	*apuralyi, yapuralyi*
Pitjantjatjara	*ngalpinka, walukara, ngapari, aparuma*
Warlpiri	*yirrkanngarli, yalparalyi*

Large tree. **Bark** smooth, whitish (sometimes streaked with red). **Leaves** dull green. Attractive creamy **flowers**. Usually flowers in November.

Habitat: More or less restricted to banks and beds of sandy watercourses.

Uses: A small lerp or scale insect (*Psylla eucalypti* [?]) feeds off sap in the leaves and excretes sugars in the form of white, sweet scales which are gathered in large numbers and eaten with relish. Another small lerp insect exudes excess sugars as a honey-like liquid which drips onto loosely attached old bark. This is stripped from the tree and soaked in water to make a sweet drink. The most favoured grub is the larva of a large cossid moth often found in trunks. Larvae of hepialid moth (*Trictena argentata*) are obtained from the roots; native bee colonies are often found in hollow trunks.

The river red gum also provides: coolamons from its roots, boles or bark; firewood; a favoured ash for pituri; children's toys; hair ornaments from seed capsules; necklaces from yellow flower caps. Branches are often used for shelters and to form mats on the ground for meat and other food. Leaves can be chewed to hide the smell of a forbidden food or drink on the breath. Portions of bark are sometimes steeped in water to produce a medicinal drink or wash.

Ref: *Bushfires & Bushtucker* p. 165

COOLIBAH
Eucalyptus coolabah* ssp. *arida* and *E. victrix
Family: Myrtaceae

Alyawarr	*ankerr, ankerrmern*
Anmatyerr	*ankerrmern, aley* (seed), *ankerrayt* (grub: E. Anm.)
E. Arrernte	*ankerre*
W. Arrernte	*ankerre*
Kaytetye	*atnkerre, aleye* (seed), *ankerrayte* (grub)
Pintupi	*ankarra* (?)
Pitjantjatjara	*ankara*
Warlpiri	*karrawari, karrkala-payipayi* (gall), *wankilinyi* (grub), *wangkilinyi* (grub), *wapilingki, yurrunyu* (seeds)

Variable tree 7–12 m. Normally all but upper branches is covered with dark, flaky but persistent **bark**. (But in *E. victrix*, occurring in north-west quarter of area, bark is usually restricted to lower metre of trunk; upper bark smooth and white, similar to ghost gum.) **Flowers** creamy white, insignificant. **Nuts** fragile, fall quickly. Flowering often occurs in January; seeds are formed soon after.

Habitat: Restricted to clayey or silty soils which are periodically flooded.

Uses: Seeds are an important food source for Arandic peoples where the tree is abundant. The tree can flower even in fairly dry times so seeds are often available when other seeds are scarce. Edible grubs are sometimes found in the wood; hollow trunks are common, and harbour native bee colonies, birds' nests, etc. Dry bark and twigs produce ash for pituri. Water is obtained from the roots.

Ref: *Bushfires & Bushtucker* p. 185

WATER MALLEE, RED MALLEE
Eucalyptus eucentrica
Family: Myrtaceae

Pitjantjatjara *ngapari, pulura*

Mallee around 5 m with some rough bark at base. **Buds** distinctive, with long pointed cap. **Flowers** creamy coloured. **Fruits** hard and thick. Flowers in winter or spring.

Habitat: Most common south of Alice Springs, but scattered populations occur further north. Always on or near limestone.

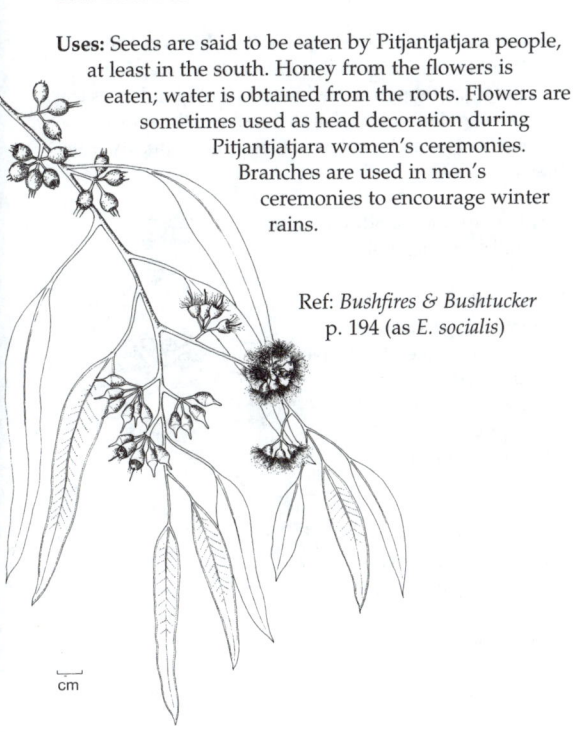

Uses: Seeds are said to be eaten by Pitjantjatjara people, at least in the south. Honey from the flowers is eaten; water is obtained from the roots. Flowers are sometimes used as head decoration during Pitjantjatjara women's ceremonies. Branches are used in men's ceremonies to encourage winter rains.

Ref: *Bushfires & Bushtucker* p. 194 (as *E. socialis*)

BLUE MALLEE
Eucalyptus gamophylla
Family: Myrtaceae

Alyawarr	*lweperr*
E. Anmatyerr	*uleperr*
W. Anmatyerr	*alhelp*
E. Arrernte	*uleperre, alhelpe*
Kaytetye	*lweperre*
Pintupi	*warrilyu, yilyulpa*
Pitjantjatjara	*warilyu* (leaves), *altarpa* (?)
Warlpiri	*warrilyi, yilangkiyi, yilangkurunyu, yirlangkurrunyu*

About 3 m. **Foliage** bluish-green. Broad **leaves** fused together at base are actually juvenile leaves retained on adult plant, although sometimes normal gum leaves can also be seen. **Flowers** creamy white, usually appear October or November. New leaves appear quickly from base after fire.

Habitat: Spinifex sandplains and sandhills, spinifex hills.

Uses: Seeds are eaten by Anmatyerr, Alyawarr and S. Warlpiri peoples: they have a pleasant nutty flavour with a faint hint of eucalyptus. Seeds are held in the nuts for six months or more and are available when other plant foods are scarce. Nuts are dried in the sun until they release seed, which is cleaned and ground into an edible paste. Flowers are said to yield honey; water is sometimes obtained from the roots.

Ref: *Bushfires & Bushtucker* p. 187

SNAPPY GUM
Eucalyptus leucophloia
Family: Myrtaceae

Alyawarr	*arlketh*
E. Anmatyerr	*arlketh*
Kaytetye	*arlkethe*
Pintupi	*ka<u>nta</u>nti, ngula<u>n</u>pa*
Warlpiri	*nurrku, wumparlpa* (?)

Small tree about 5 m, sometimes with mallee form. **Bark** white but often spotted black.

Habitat: Spinifex gravelly rises, in extreme north of the area.

Uses: A decoction of the bright yellow inner portion of the bark is used as a medicinal wash for most ailments. Wood is used for making digging scoops. Dead wood is readily broken into conveniently sized portions and is much favoured as firewood.

Ref: *Bushfires & Bushtucker* p. 188

DESERT BLOODWOOD
Eucalyptus opaca (a.k.a. *Corymbia opaca*)
Family: Myrtaceae

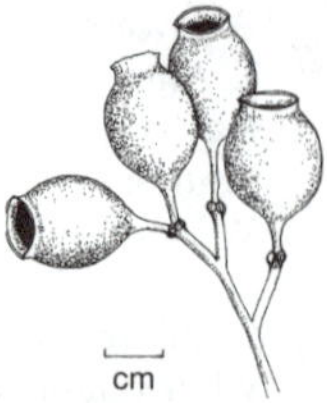

Alyawarr	*arrkerakw, arrkernk*
Anmatyerr	*arrkernk*
E. Arrernte	*arrkernke*
W. Arrernte	*arrkernke*
Kaytetye	*arrke*
Pintupi	*arrkinki, murrmurrpa, walytji, wulupu, yarrkinki*
Pitjantjatjara	*itara, muur-muurpa, tjuta*
Warlpiri	*wirrkali, wurrkali, yurrkali, yurrkulju* (nectar-bearing flowers)

GALL (BUSH COCONUT, BLOODWOOD APPLE)

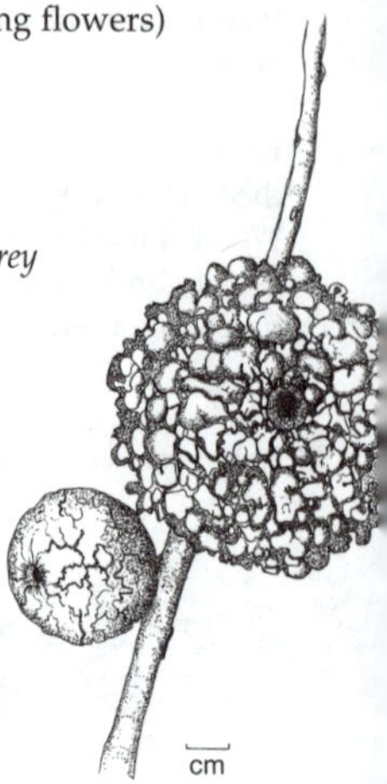

Alyawarr	*kathip*
E. Anmatyerr	*arrkwerlpwerlp, mangarrey*
W. Anmatyerr	*kerlpankwel*
E. Arrernte	*arrkipangkwerle*
W. Arrernte	*arrkernkunpe*
Kaytetye	*arrkwerlpwerlpe*
Pintupi	*nanukitji, wanpanpi*
Pitjantjatjara	*angura*
Warlpiri	*jakarla-payi-payi, kanta, kajipu, mangarrayi, mawu* (liquid in gall), *yanturi*

GALL GRUB

Alyawarr	*lyerrew*
E. Anmatyerr	*kathip*
Kaytetye	*katheype*
Warlpiri	*warnparnpi*

RESIN (KINO)

Alyawarr	*arrkiper*
E. Anmatyerr	*arrkiper*
W. Anmatyerr	*arrkeper*
Kaytetye	*arrkeypere, arnenpe*
Warlpiri	*mijilypa*

TREE

To 12 m. **Bark** pale brown, scaly, extends up to twigs. **Flowers** pale yellow. **Fruits** large, thick walled. **Gall** apple-sized, usually with rough exterior when mature (smooth form occurs in Western Desert area). When mature gall is opened, a grub about 4 cm long can be found attached to inner wall. Flowers in autumn or winter. (*E. chippendalei*, a similar species, has larger, more rounded fruits.)

Habitat: Scattered trees occur in all habitats but driest sandy areas. (*E. chippendalei* found in western third of area, growing only on sand dune crests.)

Uses: Bush coconuts found on this tree are eaten throughout the area. Inner portion of the gall is white edible flesh about 1 cm thick, similar to a coconut. Sweet white lerp scale is sometimes found on the leaves; in good seasons flowers produce copious honey. This is a favourite home of native bees (*Trigona* species), whose honey ('sugarbag') is probably the most sought-after delicacy in Central Australia. Resin (kino) exuding from wounds on the trunk is mixed with water and applied to sore eyes and lips, wounds, burns and sores; small amounts are sometimes drunk for sore throats. If kino is not readily available, burnt bark is mixed with fat and applied to burns. Red sap is used as a tanning agent for kangaroo-skin waterbags; wood is used for certain implements and dead wood is one of the most favoured firewoods, burning with a steady, hot flame. Fruit capsules are sometimes used as hair decorations, necklaces or toys. Leafy sprigs are often placed under armbands and legbands during ceremonies.

Ref: *Bushfires & Bushtucker* p. 189

ROUND-FRUITED MALLEE
Eucalyptus oxymitra
Family: Myrtaceae

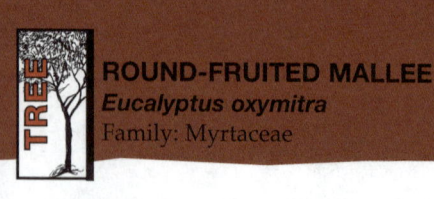

Pitjantjatjara *altarrpa* (?), *tjitulpuru*
Warlpiri *juturlpuru*

Mallee 4–6 m. **Bark** smooth, usually whitish. **Leaves** thick, leathery, grey-green. **Flowers** large, attractive, yellow. Usually flowers in summer.

Habitat: With spinifex in red sand or on rocky hillsides, in the south-western third of the area.

Uses: Edible lerp scale is sometimes found on the leaves. Flowers provide honey. The large attractive nuts — *taṯu* (Pit.) — are used as hair ornaments or necklaces.

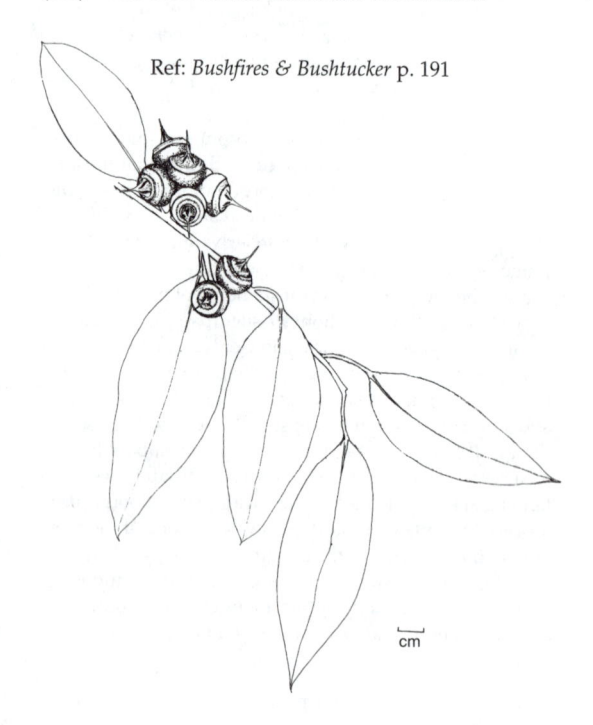

Ref: *Bushfires & Bushtucker* p. 191

RED MALLEE
Eucalyptus pachyphylla
Family: Myrtaceae

Alyawarr	*ntyeny*
E. Anmatyerr	*ntyeny*
E. Arrernte	*ntyenye*
Kaytetye	*ntyenye*
Pintupi	*tjitulpuru*
Warlpiri	*jitilypuru, juturlpuru, walyilpi, warrilyi*

Mallee 4–6 m. **Bark** smooth, pink. **Leaves** thick, leathery, bright green. **Buds** large, red. **Flowers** yellow or, more rarely, pink. Usually flowers in spring. (*E. sessilis* is very similar but has more buds on each stalk. Mainly on rocky hillsides throughout area. Not distinguished by Aboriginal people, and apparently used in same way.)

Habitat: Grows with spinifex on sandplains in the northern third of the area.

Uses: The Pintupi are reputed to eat the seeds of this plant. Honey is found in the flowers in relatively large amounts. The edible lerp scale sometimes found on the leaves is considered to be sweeter and better than that found on any other gum. Nuts are used for ornamentation and by children for spinning tops.

Ref: *Bushfires & Bushtucker* p. 192

GHOST GUM
Eucalyptus papuana
(a.k.a. *Corymbia aparrerinja*)
Family: Myrtaceae

Alyawarr	*ilwemp, lwemp*
Anmatyerr	*ilwemp, lwemp, pwernengk* (W. Anm.), *ulemp* (E. Anm.)
E. Arrernte	*ilwempe*
W. Arrernte	*ilwempe*
Kaytetye	*tyelkenhe*
Pintupi	*kilkilpa*
Pitjantjatjara	*para, pilpira*
Warlpiri	*wapurnungku*

Striking tree, 6–15 m. **Trunk** straight, smooth, white; powdery to touch. Drooping **branches**. **Leaves** bright green, somewhat twisted. **Flowers** pale yellow, usually inconspicuous. **Capsules** soft and brittle. Generally flowers in mid-summer, but same tree rarely flowers every year.

Habitat: Woodland: usually near watercourses, in sand below hills or on rocky hillsides.

Uses: A type of honey is obtained from peeling bark; large edible grubs are found in the trunk. Living bark is easily and quickly stripped from the trunk and commonly used to make bark dishes. Wood is sometimes used for implements. Naturally hollow branches are used as a type of trumpet in love magic by Arrernte people: not a musical instrument as such, but simply to intensify the sound of a love song. Red sap from wounds in the trunk is applied to burns, sores and wounds, and also sometimes mixed with kangaroo dung to form a cement to repair cracked bowls and other wooden implements. Strong in Aboriginal mythology. Individual trees are often considered to represent Dreamtime ancestral beings.

Ref: *Bushfires & Bushtucker* p. 193

WILD FIG, DESERT FIG
Ficus platypoda var. *minor*
Family: Moraceae

Alyawarr	*tywerrk*
W. Anmatyerr	*tywerrk*
E. Anmatyerr	*utyerrk*
E. Arrernte	*utyerrke*
W. Arrernte	*tywerrke*
Kaytetye	*tywerrke*
Pintupi	*il̲i, witjirrki, yil̲i*
Pitjantjatjara	*il̲i*
Warlpiri	*wijirrki*

Up to 4 m high, 6 m in diameter. **Bark** grey and smooth. **Leaves** glossy green, leathery. **Fruits** mature from yellow to red-brown. In good seasons aerial roots often descend from branches. Fruit produced at any time of year, dependent on rainfall.

Habitat: Throughout area but restricted to hills — usually in gorges and other sheltered areas. Sometimes found growing out of rocky cliffs with roots extending as far as 50 m down to moist areas.

Uses: An important food plant throughout the area. Ripe fruits are tart but favoured; large amounts can be gathered from one bush. Early European settlers sometimes used the fruit for jam. When other plant foods are scarce, dry fruits are collected from under the bush and ground to a paste which is eaten raw or rolled into balls for later use.

Ref: *Bushfires & Bushtucker* p. 196

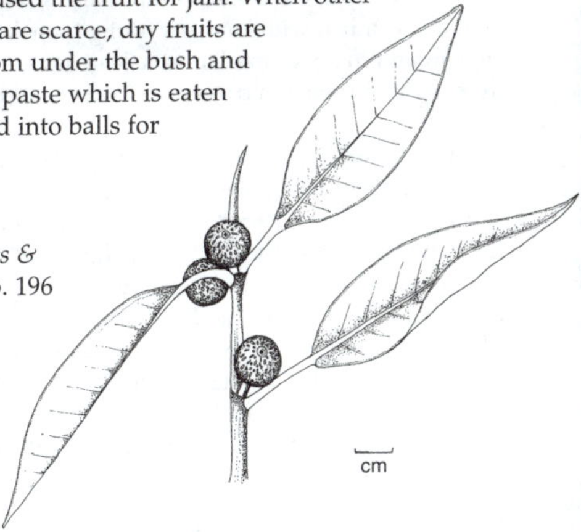

BEEFWOOD
Grevillea striata
Family: Proteaceae

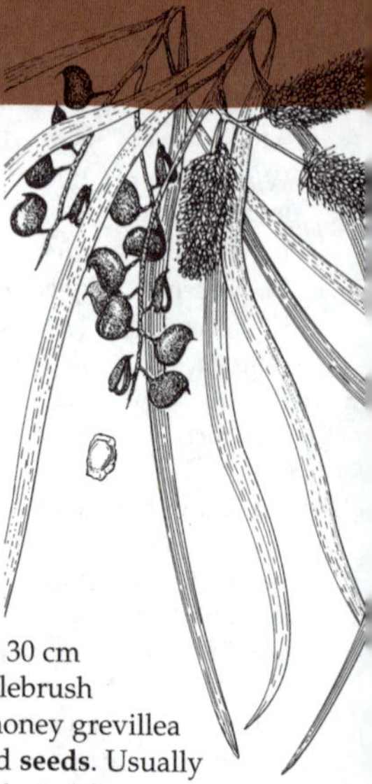

Alyawarr	*irltenty, iyltenty*
Anmatyerr	*ltyenty*
E. Anmatyerr	*iyltenty*
E. Arrernte	*irltentye, ltyentye*
W. Arrernte	*ltyantye*
Kaytetye	*peyltentye*
Pintupi	*yiltilypa*
Pitjantjatjara	*iltilpa*
Warlpiri	*yiltilypa, yilykinji* (?)

To 10 m high. **Bark** dark, rough. **Leaves** pale green, leathery, about 30 cm long or longer. Creamy white bottlebrush **flowers** produce **pods** similar to honey grevillea (*G. juncifolia*, p. 133). Large winged **seeds**. Usually flowers in November regardless of rainfall.

Habitat: Scattered trees occur in most communities.

Uses: Warlpiri are reputed to eat the seed; bark ash is used with pituri. A dark reddish kino often exudes from insect wounds in the trunk; Warlpiri and Arandic peoples heat it and mix it with kangaroo dung to make a hafting cement and to repair implements. Kino is also dissolved in water and used as a dressing for sores and burns.

The itchy grub or processionary caterpillar (larva of the bag shelter moth, *Onchrogaster* species) commonly infests this tree. They are covered in irritant hairs, and hair in their dung can also cause intense itching and swelling. The fine silken nest covering may be carefully removed and cleaned, sometimes soaked with mothers' milk, then placed on burns. Even severe burns treated in this way are said to heal rapidly. In times of absolute necessity Pitjantjatjara people may eat the grub: hairs are singed off, but there is still some irritation of the mouth and throat.

Ref: *Bushfires & Bushtucker* p. 202

NORTHERN CORKWOOD, BOOTLACE TREE
Hakea chordophylla
Family: Proteaceae

Alyawarr	*alwenp, ntywey*
Anmatyerr	*ntywey, untyey, ntyweyamp* (honey: E. Anm.)
E. Arrernte	*untyeye*
Kaytetye	*eytatne, ntyeyampe* (honey)
Pintupi	*piruwa*
Warlpiri	*piriwa, nguyu-parnta*

About 5 m. **Stems** and **branches** twisted. **Bark** distinctive: thick, corky. **Leaves** smooth, cylindrical, up to 45 cm long. Hairless yellow **flowers** produce hard woody capsules containing two large-winged **seeds**. (*H. suberea*, p. 178, has hairy flowers and shorter leaves. Both species given same Aboriginal name.) Usually flowers in spring.

Habitat: Scattered trees in most communities, in the northern third of the area.

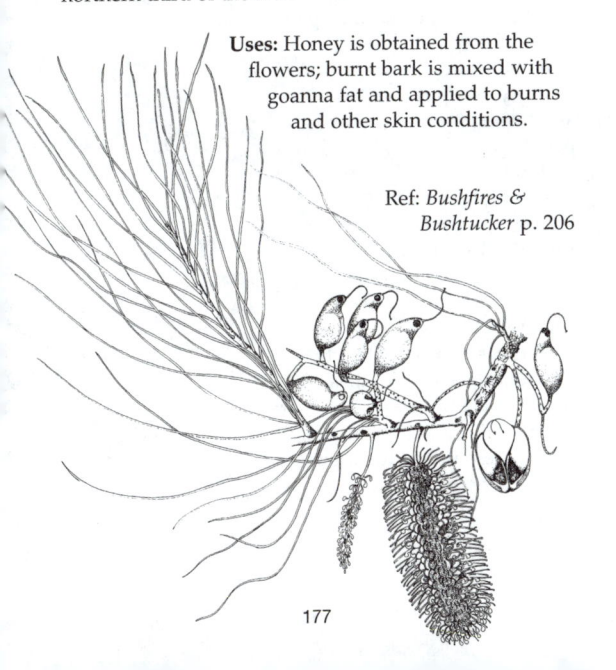

Uses: Honey is obtained from the flowers; burnt bark is mixed with goanna fat and applied to burns and other skin conditions.

Ref: *Bushfires & Bushtucker* p. 206

FORK-LEAFED CORKWOOD and LONG-LEAFED CORKWOOD

Hakea divaricata (and *H. suberea*)
Family: Proteaceae

Alyawarr	*ntywey-arengk*
Anmatyerr	*untyey, ntywey*
W. Arrernte	*ntyweye*
Kaytetye	*eytatne*
Pintupi	*piruwa*
Pitjantjatjara	*piruwa, witjinti, ularama*
Warlpiri	*kumpalpa, nguyu-parnta, parawuju, piriwa, puraja, yarrkampi*

Small gnarled tree to 7 m. Characteristic thick, corky **bark**. **Leaves** smooth, branched. **Flowers** yellow-green. **Fruits** woody, containing two winged seeds. (*H. suberea* differs only in its slightly hairy, unbranched leaves and tendency to grow on hillsides. Not generally distinguished by Aborigines, and used in same way.) Flowering often occurs in early spring but depends on rainfall.

Habitat: Trees scattered in woodland communities, usually on river flats. Non-spinifex hills.

Uses: Seeds are eaten by Warlpiri and Pitjantjatjara people without preparation. Honey is sucked from the flowers, or they are steeped in water to make a sweet blackish-coloured drink, said sometimes to have a slightly alcoholic effect. Bark ash is used to treat burns (Pit.) and sore tongues, lips and gums of children. Sometimes applied to nipples during breastfeeding.

Ref: *Bushfires & Bushtucker* p. 207

FLAT-LEAVED HAKEA, DOGWOOD HAKEA
Hakea macrocarpa
Family: Proteaceae

E. Anmatyerr	*ntyarleyarleng*
Kaytetye	*ntyarleyarlenge*
Pintupi	*wanukuṯa*
Warlpiri	*watikinpi, yanjalingki, yinjalingkalingi, yukunji*

Similar to northern corkwood (*H. chordophylla*, p. 177) except for flat, leathery **leaves** and softly hairy **flowers**. Same general appearance as dogwood (*Acacia coriacea*, p. 154) and occurs in same areas. Flowers usually produced in July.

Uses: Honeysuckle flowers, prolific in good seasons, are steeped in water to dissolve the blackish honey and make a sweet drink. Burnt bark is used for decoration. This tree has ritual significance for Warlpiri people and features in the Snake Dreaming.

Ref: *Bushfires & Bushtucker* p. 210

PALM VALLEY PALM, CABBAGE PALM
Livistona mariae ssp. *mariae*
Family: Palmae

W. Arrernte	*rrangkeye*
Pintupi	*aranki*

Stately palm to 25 m high. **Leaves** broad, fan-like. **Seeds** rounded, about the size of a marble.

Habitat: A rare relict plant restricted to an area south of Hermannsburg, mostly within Finke Gorge National Park.

Uses: Growing hearts of palms are often eaten in Northern Australia, and known as millionaire's cabbage because removal of the edible portion results in the death of the palm. There are conflicting reports as to whether this palm was used as food by W. Arrernte people in the past. The Palm Valley palm features strongly in Aboriginal mythology, including that of several peoples who do not have stands of the palm in their own country.

Ref: *Bushfires & Bushtucker* p. 222

CYCAD PALM
Macrozamia macdonnellii
Family: Zamiaceae

E. Arrernte	*atywekekwerle*
W. Arrernte	*tywekekwerle*

Small palm-like plant about 2 m. **Fronds** similar to those of date palm. **Seeds** about size and shape of an egg.

Habitat: Very rare. Small scattered populations throughout Macdonnell Ranges, in sheltered valleys and gorges on rocky hillsides.

Uses: Seeds are not eaten (unlike those of closely related species in other parts of the continent) for two probable reasons. Firstly, the plant is quite rare and does not often produce large amounts of seeds. Secondly, removal of the highly toxic principles found in the seeds is extremely difficult. Smaller seeds found on other species apparently lose their toxic principles when thoroughly roasted, but this would probably not work with larger seeds. There is also a complicated leaching procedure involving running water, not practicable in arid areas. Rock wallabies can always be found near this plant.

Ref: *Bushfires & Bushtucker* p. 223

NATIVE WILLOW, APRICOT TREE
Pittosporum phylliraeoides
Family: Pittosporaceae

Alyawarr	*ampwerrety, welterr*
E. Anmatyerr	*welterr, anawert, atnawert*
W. Anmatyerr	*anawert*
E. Arrernte	*atnawerte*
W. Arrernte	*tnawerte*
Kaytetye	*eltwerreye*
Pitjantjatjara	*alita, kumpalypa*
Warlpiri	*ngamari, pawurlirri, wirnpirarri, yarnawurdu*

Attractive tree or small shrub, 2–7 m. **Bark** rough (at least at base). Drooping **foliage**; leaves smooth, green, somewhat leathery. **Flowers** pale yellow. **Fruit** orange, containing several sticky red **seeds**; sticky substance is extremely bitter. Fruits generally produced after rain, but most commonly found in spring or summer.

Habitat: In woodlands near rivers or on foothills. Never very abundant.

Uses: Pitjantjatjara are reputed to grind the seeds for use as a poultice. In other areas of Australia a decoction of the leaves is drunk for colds or used as a medicinal wash. A compress of warmed leaves is also said to induce milk flow for new mothers. Personal experience shows the oils coating the seed to be a beneficial rub for sore muscles and sprains. Seeds are reputed to be eaten in other parts of Australia, but not in this area.

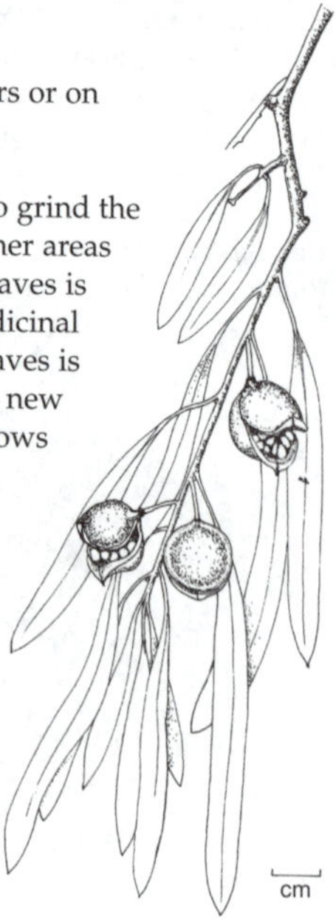

Ref: *Bushfires & Bushtucker*
p. 246

QUANDONG, NATIVE PEACH, PEACH TREE
Santalum acuminatum
Family: Santalaceae

W. Anmatyerr	*mangart*
E. Arrernte	*pmerlpe, pmwerlpe*
W. Arrernte	*pmwerlpe*
Pintupi	*mangata, walku*
Pitjantjatjara	*kuuturu, mangata, walku, wayanu, witirrpa* (seed)
Warlpiri	*mangarda, mangarta*

Small tree or shrub up to 4 m. **Bark** rough, dark and light green. **Leaves** somewhat leathery. **Flowers** small, greenish. **Fruit** bright red and fleshy, enclosing round pitted stone about size of a marble. (There is also a yellow-fruited form.) Plant is a root parasite, at least in its younger stages. Fruits usually ripen in September or October, depending on rainfall. Being fire sensitive and heavily grazed by stock, especially camels, it is now becoming a rare plant.

Habitat: Usually in limestone areas, often near watercourses, salt lakes or hills, only in the south-western third of the area.

Uses: A traditional staple food, much sought after throughout its range. Fruit is tart but pleasant tasting when ripe, and is highly nutritious, with twice as much vitamin C as an orange. Dried fruits collected from under the tree are easily reconstituted in water. Excess fruit is pounded, made into cakes, dried and stored for later use. The kernels are also nutritious — 25 per cent protein, 70 per cent oil — but are apparently rarely utilised, and then only after roasting the seeds. A paste made from ground seeds is considered a powerful medicine and rubbed into the body as a liniment for general ailments. It has recently been found to contain an important antibiotic. Wood, especially from the roots, is used to make bowls and other objects (nowadays animal carvings and artefacts for sale). Water is often trapped in hollows in the trunk and sucked out with a type of straw made from the bark. Children use the seeds for marbles.

Ref: *Bushfires & Bushtucker* p. 259

SUPPLEJACK, SUPLEJACK
Ventilago viminalis
Family: Rhamnaceae

Alyawarr	atnyer
Anmatyerr	atnyer, anyer
E. Arrernte	atnyere
W. Arrernte	tnyere
Kaytetye	atnyere
Warlpiri	nganyiri, walakarri

Shrub or tree, about 5 m. Vine-like when young. Mature plant usually has several intertwined **trunks** with dark scaly **bark**. **Leaves** drooping, bright green. **Flowers** insignificant, pale green. Winged **seeds** are wind-borne.

Habitat: Rare or absent south of Macdonnell Ranges. Found in woodlands and low hills but rarely abundant.

Uses: A sweet white gum — *atnyerampe* (Arr.) — often found seeping from insect wounds in the trunk during spring, is a favoured food. Small spears are sometimes made from the stem. Bark ash is used for pituri. 'Sugar bags' (native bee colonies) are sometimes found in hollows in the trunk. Thick foliage is considered useful shade. Elsewhere in Australia, the roots and bark are used to make a decoction considered useful for various ailments and even used as hair restorer!

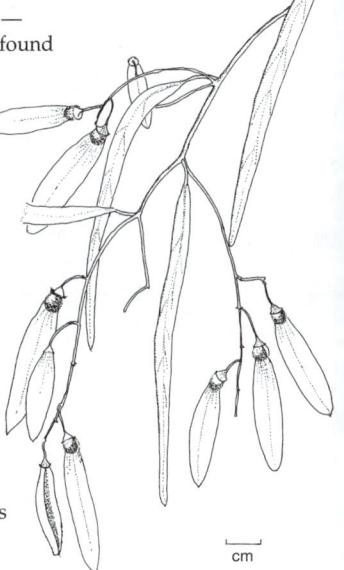

Ref: *Bushfires & Bushtucker* p. 295

VINES, PARASITES and FUNGI

VINE

NATIVE GOOSEBERRY, ULCARDO MELON, NATIVE MELON, NATIVE CUCUMBER
Cucumis melo ssp. *agrestis*
Family: Cucurbitaceae

Alyawarr	*lkwart*
Anmatyerr	*lkwart, ilkwart, ulkart* (E. Anm.)
Arrernte	*ilkartwe*
Kaytetye	*elkwarte, kwelkarte*
Warlpiri	*ngalparanpa*

Annual twining creeper, rough to touch. **Flowers** small, yellow. **Fruits** green, maturing to yellowish colour. Immature fruits well camouflaged amongst leaves until they reach maturity. Growth occurs in summer after rain; fruit persist on vine for months after leaves have fallen.

Habitat: Mostly restricted to extreme east of area. Grows only in heavy clay soils, on treeless clay plains or on floodouts.

Uses: Fruit is highly favoured wherever it is found. The skin is bitter when immature and the fruit is not much eaten until the skin has lost its green colour and bitterness. It keeps well, so is available for several months of the year but mostly (because of its limited distribution) to Arandic peoples.

Ref: *Bushfires & Bushtucker* p. 155

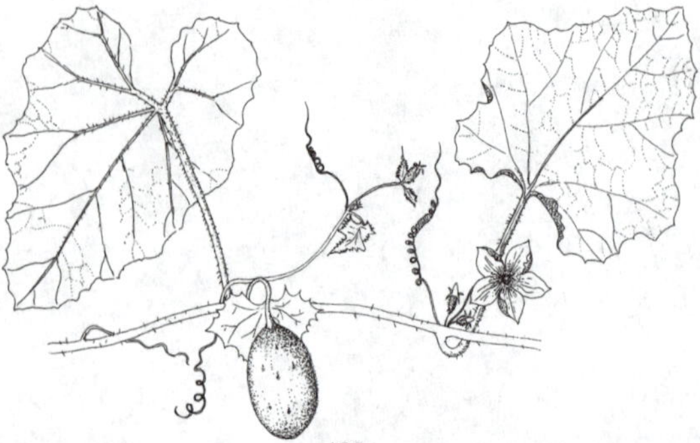

BUSH POTATO, DESERT YAM
Ipomoea costata
Family: Convolvulaceae

VINE

Alyawarr	*anaty*
Anmatyerr	*anaty, anek, nalal* (flower: E. Anm.)
E. Arrernte	*anatye*
W. Arrernte	*natye*
Kaytetye	*anatye, nalale* (flower)
Pintupi	*ala, altjirrpa, pitjara, yala, yaltjirrpa*
Warlpiri	*yarla, karnti, papirta, puurda, yaljirrpa, yangurnungu,* grub: *yarla-pama*; flower: *jijardu, jirtardu*; leaves: *pijara* (ear); rooting vine: *ngamarna*; tuber under vine: *mardu, wirlirnpangi*; tuber from roots: *watarlapi, wunju*

cm

Viny shrub, usually about 1 m. Longer **branches** creep on ground. Often roots at nodes. Sometimes climbs up trees. **Leaves** smooth, green, leathery. **Flowers** large, showy; pink with red throat. Flowers and new growth mostly produced during summer months after rain.

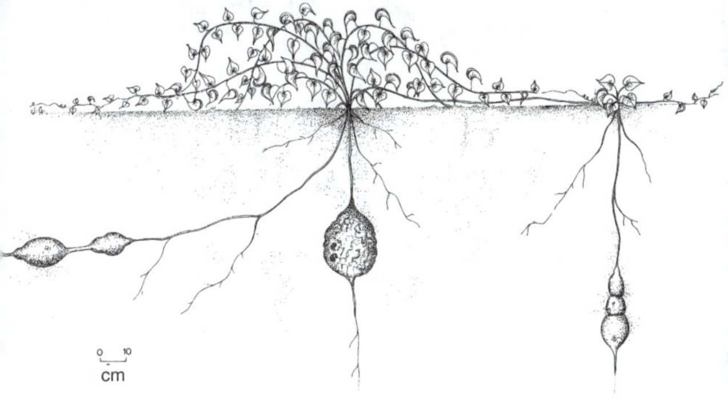

0 10
cm

Habitat: Usually found on spinifex sandplains; rarely in areas near hills or under mulga, in the northern third of the area.

Uses: A staple food throughout its range. The tubers taste sweetish — similar to cultivated sweet potato (also an *Ipomoea*) — and are usually very juicy. Three types of tuber can be found under any one bush:
1) In good seasons long runners send down roots up to a metre into soft sand, to where the tubers can be found.
2) Tubers are produced on the parent plant's lateral roots, up to 3 m distant from the base. They are produced in all seasons, but are harder to find. Aboriginal people search for cracks in the ground or hit the ground with a digging stick, listening for a hollow sound.
3) This type is usually found directly below the mature plant. They are large but usually quite old, so they are hard, woody and of little value as a food. They are probably eaten only in times of extreme hardship.

Ref: *Bushfires & Bushtucker* p. 214

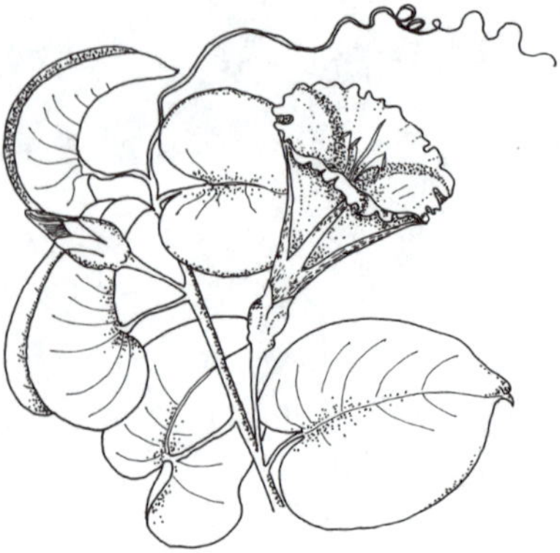

NATIVE MORNING GLORY
Ipomoea muelleri
Family: Convolvulaceae

VINE

Alyawarr	*anaytapaytap, twatywert*
Anmatyerr	*katyetarr, kwatyetarr*
E. Anmatyerr	*atywert-atywert*
W. Anmatyerr	*twatyert, tatyetarr (?), katyetarr (?), kwatyetarr (?)*
Kaytetye	*atywert-atywerte*
Warlpiri	*karlampi-jurtujurtu, ngarlangkartapi, yutajiti*

Similar to bush potato (*I. costata*, p. 189) but smaller in all respects. **Stems** weak, often twining. **Seeds** hairy.

Habitat: Throughout area, but more abundant north of Alice Springs where it is usually found in red, sandy or clayey soils, usually under mulga.

Uses: Warlpiri and Anmatyerr people eat the roots, possibly as an undesirable drought food. The Warlpiri are reputed also to eat the seeds.

Ref: *Bushfires & Bushtucker* p. 216

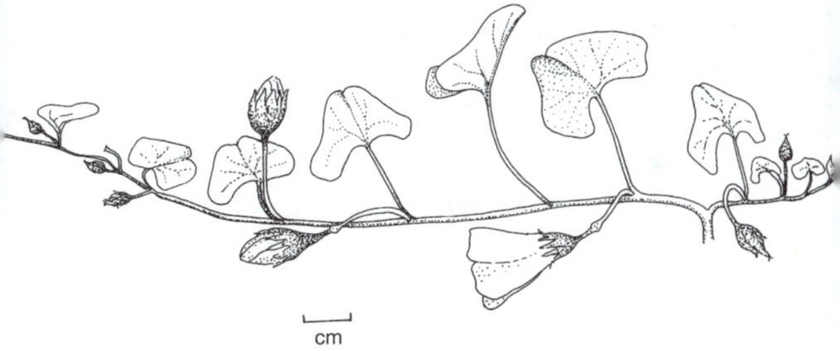

BUSH BANANA, SILKY PEAR
Marsdenia australis
Family: Asclepiadaceae

Alyawarr	alkwarrer
Anmatyerr	alangkw, parl (W. Anm.)
	alkwarrer (E. Anm.)
E. Arrernte	altyeye
W. Arrernte	altyeye
Kaytetye	alkwarreye
Pintupi	ipala, ipalu, kulurrpa, langa, yipala, muulpu, unturrngu, utiralya, wilypa, yipala, yipalu, yunturrngu
Pitjantjatjara	ngunala, unturngu, utiralya
Warlpiri	yuparli, murlku-kari (?), ngakaparla (?), purrputuru (?)

FRUITS

Anmatyerr	alangkw, parl (W. Anm.)
	alkwarrer (E. Anm.)
E. Arrernte	alangkwe
W. Arrernte	langkwe
Kaytetye	alkwarreye
Pitjantjatjara	kalkula
Warlpiri	yangardurrku, yurnturrngu

FLOWERS

Alyawarr	rlkwanty
Anmatyerr	ilkwanty, ulkanty
E. Arrernte	ulkantyerrknge
Kaytetye	erlkwantye
Warlpiri	nyiingka (bud)

LEAVES

Alyawarr	pwelk, unel
Anmatyerr	altyey, unel
E. Arrernte	altyeye
Kaytetye	altyeye
Warlpiri	parla

EDIBLE ROOTS

Alyawarr	anngety, atnety
E. Anmatyerr	atnety
E. Arrernte	atnetye

VINE

Kaytetye	*atnetye*
Pintupi	*unala, yunala*
Pitjantjatjara	*atangka, ngunala*

Woody, winding vine which climbs up other trees and shrubs; often difficult to see amongst their leaves. **Flowers** creamy. **Leaves** green. Exudes a white latex when bruised. Mature fruit open to release numerous **seeds** with light feathery plumes attached to one end (similar to a dandelion) which can be carried long distances by wind. Grows quickly after rain; fruits ripen about a month later.

Habitat: Most habitats, but rare in south-west corner, probably because of overgrazing by rabbits.

Uses: An important and favoured food throughout the area. Only the stems and fine roots are not eaten at some stage. Sweet flowers, young fruits and young leaves are eaten raw. Mature fruits — mainly seeds and plumes — are either cooked and eaten whole, or the seeds are discarded and the thick outer rind is eaten raw. Older leaves are steamed; roots are apparently only eaten in times of hardship.

Ref: *Bushfires & Bushtucker* p. 224

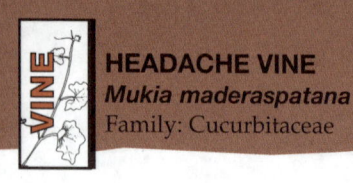

HEADACHE VINE
Mukia maderaspatana
Family: Cucurbitaceae

Anmatyerr	*ankeyankey* (?), *lkwartelkwart* (W. Anm.)
E. Arrernte	*ilkwerte-ilkwerte*
Pintupi	*papawitilpa*
Pitjantjatjara	*kalpil-kalpilpa* (climbing plants in general), *papawitilpa*

Short-lived climbing creeper, rough to touch. Smooth, rounded **berries** change from green to yellow, then bright red.

Habitat: Most habitats, although reduced by being eaten by cattle.

Uses: Leaves are pulped, moistened with a little water, and used as a cold compress to relieve headaches and induce sleep (Pit.). Warlpiri people sometimes use the stems as a thread for necklaces. The plant has various medicinal uses throughout much of Asia.

Ref: *Bushfires & Bushtucker* p. 228

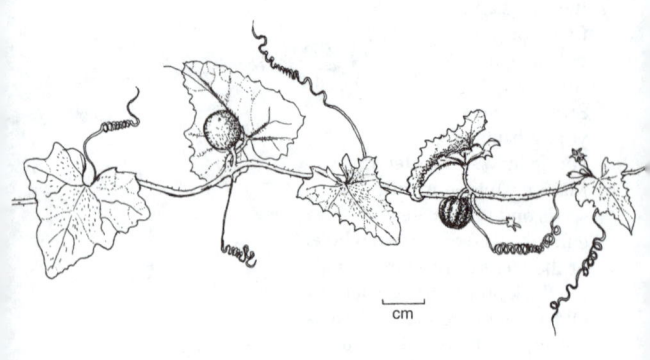

KANGAROO BALLS VINE
Mukia sp. *c* (a.k.a *Mukia A50961 Glen Helen Station*)
Family: Cucurbitaceae

VINE

Alyawarr	*aherrarleth*
E. Anmatyerr	*aherrarleth, aherrarlweth*
E. Arrernte	*ilkwerte-ilkwerte*
Kaytetye	*aherralwethe*
Warlpiri	*yukuri, yulkardi*

Creeping or scrambling plant with perennial rootstock. **Foliage** is rough to touch, especially undersides of leaves. Small yellow **flowers** produce bitter, greenish **fruit**. Similar to native gooseberry (*Cucumis melo* ssp. *agrestis*, p. 188) but has smaller flowers and leaves and less-rounded fruit.

Habitat: Mulga communities in the northern half of the area.

Uses: Pulp from the fruit is rubbed on sore eyes and sores on the skin, or on the head to relieve headaches. It is considered a useful medicine throughout its range. Kangaroos love to eat this plant and can always be found nearby.

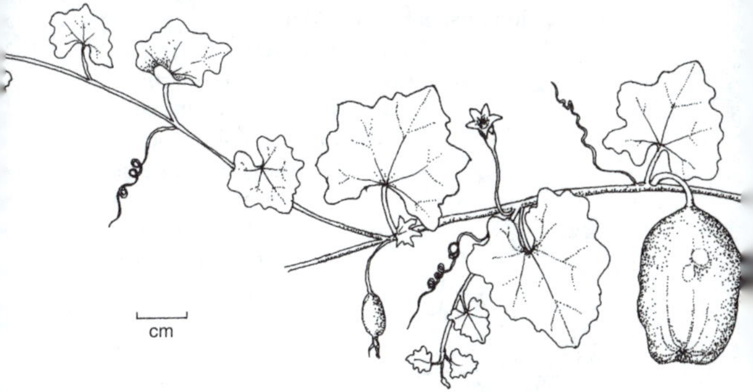

Ref: *Bushfires & Bushtucker* p. 228

VINE

SPEARBUSH, SPEARWOOD
Pandorea doratoxylon
Family: Bignoniaceae

Alyawarr	*ayenper*
E. Anmatyerr	*uyenper, ywenper*
W. Anmatyerr	*yenper*
E. Arrernte	*uyenpere*
W. Arrernte	*yenpere*
Kaytetye	*yenpere*
Pintupi	*intiti, yintiti*
Pitjantjatjara	*katji, kulata* (= spear), *urtjanpa*
Warlpiri	*winpiri, wiinpiri*

Large shrub 3–5 m high. **Stems** relatively thin, vine-like. Juvenile plants have fern-like appearance. **Flowers** creamy to brownish with purple striations in throat. **Pods** canoe-shaped.

Habitat: Restricted to rocky hills. Often severely grazed by euros and wallabies.

Uses: This is the plant most favoured for the construction of spear shafts. Many of the stems are unbranched over a considerable length, are a consistent width and combine flexibility and strength with lightness. Stems are straightened and strengthened by heating in hot sand and ashes. Shorter lengths are sometimes spliced together if longer lengths are not available.

Ref: *Bushfires & Bushtucker* p. 239

MULGA BEAN, BUSH BEAN
Rhyncharrhena linearis
Family: Asclepiadaceae

Alyawarr	pod: *wat, werrp*
E. Anmatyerr	*ngerak, aherretyepwer* (pod)
W. Anmatyerr	*ngarwek, awerretyepwer* (pod)
Arrernte	*ngerake*
Kaytetye	*werrpe* (pod and plant)
Pintupi	*puya*
Pitjantjatjara	*wintjulanypa, puya*
Warlpiri	*purlpalangi, purrpalangi*

Twining climber. **Leaves** thin. **Flowers** delicate, pink-brown. **Pods** green, bean-like, up to 20 cm long. Grows quickly from its perennial rootstock whenever moisture is available.

Habitat: Widespread, often climbs up mulga trees and can be difficult to see against foliage. One of the first plants to show again after a fire, and then much more easily spotted against burnt mulga.

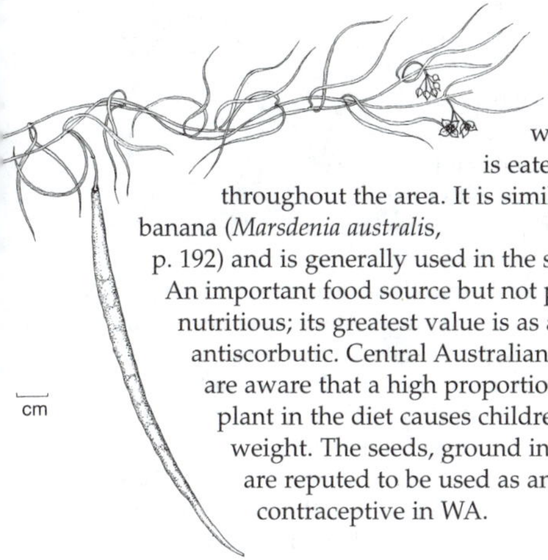

Uses: The whole plant except the somewhat woody stems is eaten throughout the area. It is similar to bush banana (*Marsdenia australis*, p. 192) and is generally used in the same way. An important food source but not particularly nutritious; its greatest value is as an antiscorbutic. Central Australian Aborigines are aware that a high proportion of this plant in the diet causes children to lose weight. The seeds, ground into a paste, are reputed to be used as an oral contraceptive in WA.

Ref: *Bushfires & Bushtucker* p. 257

SNAKE VINE
Tinospora smilacina
Family: Menispermaceae

POISONOUS

Alyawarr	*atnwerl*
Anmatyerr	*arratherrk, anwerl* (E. Anm.)
Kaytetye	*arratherrke*
Pintupi	*ngalyipi, wanta-karrpu-karrpu*
Warlpiri	*ngalyarr-ngarna, ngalyipi* (= carpet snake), *ngalyipi-pama* (grub), *wararrji*

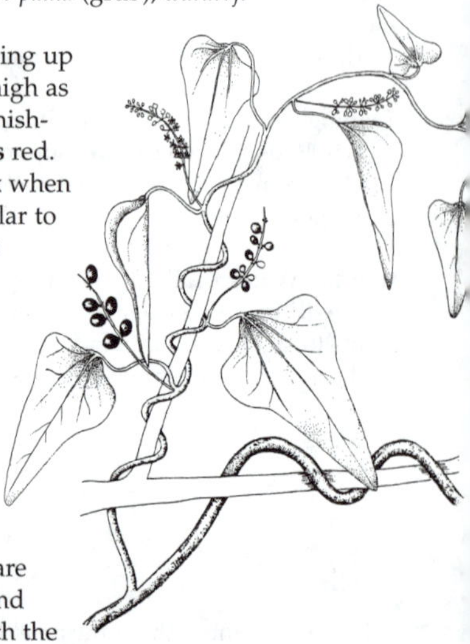

Woody twiner, climbing up trees and shrubs as high as 4–5 m. **Flowers** greenish-yellow. Mature **fruits** red. Exudes a milky **latex** when bruised. **Leaves** similar to bush potato (*Ipomoea costata*, p. 189).

Habitat: Sandplains mostly north of Aileron; also in granite areas west of Alice Springs.

Uses: Sap is dabbed on sores and leaves are placed on wounds and bound into place with the vine. Warlpiri people sometimes chew the leaves for severe colds. Sometimes stems are pounded between stones and bound around the head for headaches; they are also used for tourniquets. Stems may be used as rope for carrying purposes, for crude sandals or for tying decorative plants onto the body or onto ceremonial objects during ceremonial dances. They are also used to make designs on artefacts: stems are wrapped around an object in a certain way; the object is then placed briefly in a fire, then the stems are removed to reveal a pattern of scorched and unscorched wood. Fruits are *not* eaten.

Ref: *Bushfires & Bushtucker* p. 287

PENCIL YAM
Vigna lanceolata
Family: Fabaceae

VINE

Alyawarr	*arlatyey*
Anmatyerr	*arlatyey*
E. Arrernte	*arlatyeye, irranenye*
S. Arrernte	*irtennge*
W. Arrernte	*irlatyeye*
Kaytetye	*apeyte*
Pintupi	*atanngi, katjutarri, kutjuntu, wapiti, yatanngi*
Pitjantjatjara	*atapungkula (?), katjutari*
Warlpiri	*japirda, wapirti, ngarlajiyi, kajutari, wajaraki, yumurnunju*

Trailing herb or creeper. Sometimes covers large areas. **Leaves** bright green. **Flowers** yellow. Grows after rain at any time of year. Narrow-leafed form (with longer, thinner tubers) recognised by Warlpiri as a different species (*kajutari*).

Habitat: Woodland, watercourse, swamp. Rare or absent in south-west corner; usually found near watercourses or at base of granite hills.

Uses: The swollen roots of this plant — juicy and starchy, but with a rather bland taste — are an important food throughout its range. They are eaten raw or, more frequently, cooked in hot sand and ashes. The above-ground portion of the plant usually dies off a month or so after rain and yams are usually collected after this. Locating the tubers takes considerable skill: a knowledge of their specific habitat and the ability to recognise the remaining dry stems and leaves. As a widespread food, available for most of year, it plays an important role in the traditional economy. The plant often has buried pods like small white peanuts which are probably eaten if available.

Ref: *Bushfires & Bushtucker*
p. 296

MISTLETOE
Amyema species and *Lysiana* species
Family: Loranthaceae

Alyawarr	*amar, amapek, apweralhem, atyankern*
Anmatyerr	*amar, tyankern, ngkwerrm*
E. Anmatyerr	*aytankern, akweltyayt* (grub), *apeketyalkwarr* (fruit), *pweralhem*
E. Arrernte	*amare, angkwerrpme, atyankerne, pelyewalkarre*
W. Arrernte	*irnmare, tyankerne*
Kaytetye	*amare, aytankerne, ngkwerrme, akweltyayte* (grub), *pweralheme*
Pintupi	*miipurupa, ngantja, nganytja*
Pitjantjatjara	*ngantja, parka-parka, warilyu, nyinkini, nyirunypa*
Warlpiri	*jankirni, ngardarnkirni, ngardanykinyi, ngamari, yarrmirlpi, yulyurlpu, yunkurrmu, pawurlirri, nyanyakirri, nganangkiji,*

Mistletoes are parasites which draw all their nutrients from host plants. All Central Australian mistletoes are woody plants, usually with thick leathery **leaves** that often resemble the host plant's. On opening, **flowers** split halfway down the tube in *Lysiana* but all the way to the base in *Amyema*. One or another of the different species will be fruiting throughout the year.

Lysiana murrayi

Uses: The fruit of all except one or two Central Australian mistletoes is eaten, more for flavour than nutrition: the berry is mostly indigestible.

Ref: *Bushfires & Bushtucker* p. 125

Amyema gibberula
Hairy, with greyish cylindrical **leaves**, **Flowers** pink. **Fruits** sub-globular. Grows on *Grevillea* or *Hakea* species; widespread but rare in far east of area. **Fruit** not favoured.

Amyema maidenii
Bunched plant. **Leaves** greyish. **Flowers** greenish. **Fruit** cylindrical, maturing yellowish. Grows on acacias, usually mulga or witchetty bush, and found throughout area. **Fruit** is eaten.

Amyema preissii
Leaves yellow-green, cylindrical. **Flowers** reddish. Grows on acacias; occasionally on *Cassia* species Widespread. **Fruit** is globular, often whitish, and is eaten.

Amyema sanguinea
Drooping mistletoe. **Leaves** thick, yellow-green. **Flowers** red. Usually found on eucalypts (especially ghost gum) in north and central west. Cylindrical **fruit** is eaten.

Ref: *Bushfires & Bushtucker* pp. 126–7

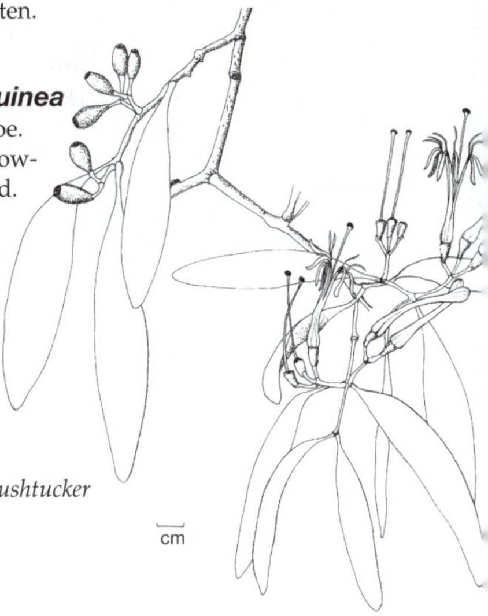

A. sanguinea

PARASITE

Lysiana exocarpi ssp. *exocarpi*
Stiff mistletoe. **Leaves** long, thin. **Flowers** red, rarely yellow. **Fruit** somewhat cylindrical (flattened on end), red or black. Usually found on acacias. **Fruit** is eaten.

Lysiana murrayi
Leaves very narrow; **flowers** greenish or yellowish. **Fruit** globular, pink or red, and is eaten. Grows mostly on acacias. Widespread, but rare or absent in far north of the area.

L. exocarpi

Lysiana spathulata
Leaves broad, often greyish-green. **Flowers** red in lower half, green above. Cylindrical **fruit** is eaten. Occurs on various plants, often *Acacia*, *Melaleuca* or *Ficus* species.

Lysiana subfalcata
Leaves flat, but long and thin. **Flowers** red and green or yellow and green. Various host plants; apparently absent in south-east corner of area. Cylindrical **fruit** is eaten.

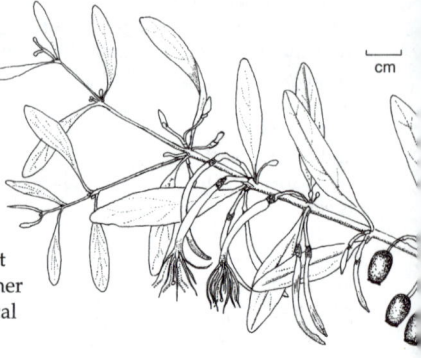

L. subfalcata

Ref: *Bushfires & Bushtucker* p. 127

NATIVE TRUFFLE, DESERT TRUFFLE
Choiromyces aboriginum, Elderia arenivaga, Mycocleandia arenacea and *M. bulundari*
Family: Tuberaceae

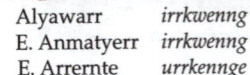

Alyawarr	*irrkwenng*
E. Anmatyerr	*irrkwenng*
E. Arrernte	*urrkennge*
W. Arrernte	*lyekemerne, werrtye*
S. Arrernte	*mantyalwerrknge*
Kaytetye	*errkwennge, pwelantere, akwerretethe*
Pintupi	*mulpu*
Pitjantjatjara	*mulpa, witita*
Warlpiri	*jinti-parnta, purlurntari, wilyiri*

White and juicy when young, becoming yellowish and wrinkled with maturity. Because there are several species involved, size and shape vary, but they are generally about as big as an apricot. Available a week or two after heavy rain, usually in cooler months.

Habitat: Spinifex sandhills and sandplains. Apparently restricted to red sandy areas, especially at base of sand dunes overlying limestone.

Uses: An important food, much sought but hard to find. Locating desert truffles requires intimate knowledge of the habitat and skill in finding small hairline cracks in the soil which indicate their presence; but in season, quite large quantities can be gathered. They are edible raw but are usually roasted in hot sand. A considerable amount of drinkable water can be wrung from fresh truffles.

Ref: *Bushfires & Bushtucker* p. 146

STALKED PUFFBALL
Podaxis pistillaris
Family: Tulostomataceae

Alyawarr	*pwenkapw, pwengapweng, arrank-arrank*
Anmatyerr	*pwek-pwek, pwek-apwek*
E. Arrernte	*pweke-apweke, irrkngenye-irrkngenye*
W. Arrernte	*kwepe-kwepe*
Kaytetye	*pwepe*
Pitjantjatjara	*ilpa̱tilpa̱ta̱, ilpa̱ta̱-ilpa̱ta̱, tilukura, ayinku̱ra, ainku̱ra, mamawa̱ra*
Warlpiri	*ngupu-ngupu*

About 10 cm high; stem 2–5 cm. At maturity, shaggy **cap** can be lifted off to reveal a mass of purplish black **spores**.

Habitat: Variety of habitats. Most common in sandy soils.

Uses: Used for decoration throughout the area. The fungus is held by the stalk while the cap is removed and the spores are brushed onto the body. Apparently mainly used by children in play: besides painting their bodies, they sometimes draw patterns or pictures on hard ground or to imitate ritual leg slashing carried out by adults during mortuary ceremonies. The N. Warlpiri are reputed to use the spores as fly repellent.

Ref: *Bushfires & Bushtucker* p. 248

SCARLET BRACKET FUNGUS
Pycnoporus coccineus
Family: Polyporaceae

Pintupi	*tjaawalirrpa*
Pitjantjatjara	*tjawalirpa, wanytji-unytjunytju*
Warlpiri	*malil-malilpa*

Upper surface is hard and somewhat rough; under-surface is porous. Mature specimens bright scarlet.

Habitat: Grows on dead wood, more or less throughout area.

Uses: Is considered poisonous if swallowed, and emits irritant smoke when burned, but is used for medicinal purposes (Pint., Pit.). May be chewed on like a teething ring, or portions are applied to the mouths of young children with skin complaints. A closely related species is used externally for various complaints in other parts of the world.

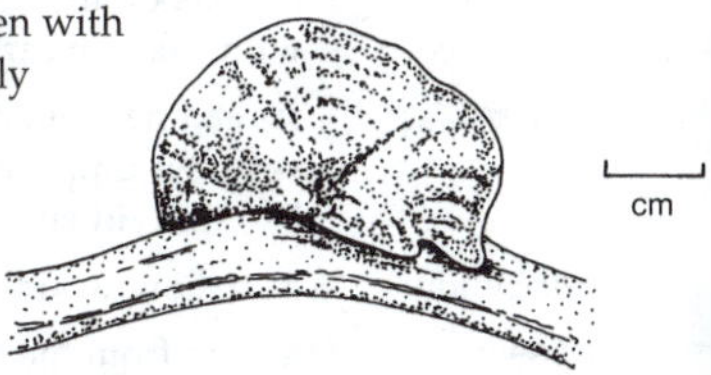

Ref: *Bushfires & Bushtucker* p. 257

GLOSSARY

a.k.a.	also known as
annual	a plant which lives for only one growing season
antiscorbutic	substance effective in preventing scurvy
Arandic	a group of Central Australian Aboriginal languages and their speakers. The Arandic languages represented in this book are: Arrernte, Western Arrernte, Anmatyerr (E. and W.), Alyawarr and Kaytetye
aril	an appendage of some seeds
basal	attached to the base
bast	inner bark
bract	specialised leaf or leaf part, situated at the base of a flower
calcareous	chalky: of, like, containing or coated with calcium carbonate
clonal	spreading from the parent plant by non-sexual multiplication to form a colony of like individuals
coolamon	a shallow wooden dish
cossid	a grub from the family Cossidae, moths with heavy bodies and narrow wings which lay eggs in trees; typically, the larvae tunnel into the timber
decoction	an extract obtained from plants by boiling them in water
floodout	an area of land where the flow of an inland river ceases to be in a well-defined channel
gall	any abnormal vegetable growth on a plant; can have many causes
gilgai	a natural soil formation characterised by a markedly undulating surface, sometimes with mounds and depressions; occurs extensively in inland Australia
glabrous	smooth, hairless

hybridisation	cross-breeding between different species, varieties etc.
infusion	an extract obtained from plants by steeping or soaking them in water
internodes	fleshy area between nodes on a stem
kino	reddish or blackish juice or gum exudation, thickened by evaporation
laterite	a reddish soil
lerp	a sweet-tasting waxy secretion found on eucalypt leaves, formed by the young of psyllids as a protection
levee	a raised riverbank created by the deposit of silt during flooding
node	a joint in a stem; a part of a stem which normally bears a leaf
perennial	a plant with a life cycle lasting more than two years
relict	a species living on in an environment which has changed from its typical environment; a survivor from the past
scree	rock detritus or gravel on a steep slope
striation	stripe or streak
sub-globular	almost spherical
tuber	a fleshy outgrowth from a root — for example a potato
viscid	sticky, adhesive or glutinous
woomera	a throwing stick for a dart or spear; gives greater range and accuracy
yandy	to separate seeds from husks and other refuse by rocking in a shallow bowl (also called a yandy)

CROSS REFERENCE OF PLANT NAMES

Page numbering — **Bold**: major entries. Roman: in-text references. *Italic*: photos.

Abutilon leucopetalum 34
   otocarpum **34**
Acacia species 201, 202
Acacia acradenia **80**, 104
   adsurgens **81**
   ancistrocarpa **82**
   aneura **87**, *121*, 150
   calcicola **153**
   colei **83**
   coriacea ssp. *seriocophylla* **154**, 179
   cowleana **83**
   cuthbertsonii **84**
   dictyophleba **92**
   elachantha **83**
   estrophiolata **155**
   farnesiana **85**
   georginae **156**
   inaequilatera **86**
   jensenii **92**
   kempeana **87**, *120*
   ligulata **89**
   lysiphloia **90**
   macdonnelliensis **157**
   maitlandii **91**
   melleodora **92**
   minyura **101**, 148
   monticola **90**
   murrayana **102**
   paraneura 150
   pruinocarpa **158**
   ramulosa **103**
   stipuligera **104**
   tenuissima 81
   tetragonophylla **105**
   validinervia **106**
   victoriae **107**, *121*
acacia, elegant **107**, *121*
acacia bush **107**, *121*
Allocasuarina decaisneana **159**
Amaranthus species **35**
Amaranthus grandiflorus **35**
   interruptus 35
   mitchellii 35

amaranthus, desert **35**
Amyema species **200 ff.**
Amyema gibberula **201**
   maidenii **201**
   preissii **201**
   sanguinea **201**
apple bush **56**, *95*
apricot tree **182**
armgrass millet **30**
ash (for pituri) 89, 134, 144, 151, 153, 154, 155, 158, 159, 165, 166, 185
Atalaya hemiglauca **160**
Austrotachardia acaciae **151**

bag shelter moth (larva) 176
banana, bush *124*, **192**, 197, 198
banana-flavoured bush tomato **73**
bats-wing coral tree **163**
bean, bush **197**
   mulga **197**
bean tree **163**
beefwood 135, **176**
bees, native 19, 165, 166, 171, 185
billy button 58
bird flower **64**
bird flower, dwarf **64**
bird-flower grevillea **132**, *119*
black boy **148**
black gidgee **158**
bloodwood, desert *122*, **170**
bloodwood apple (gall) *122*, **170**
blue
   mallee **168**
   wattle **106**
Boerhavia species **36**
Boerhavia coccinea **36**
   repleta 36
   schomburgkiana 36

bony-fruited bush tomato 77
bootlace tree 177
Brachiaria species 30, 31
Brachychiton gregorii 161
bracket fungus, scarlet 205
broom bush 145
buck spinifex 25, 26
buckbush 59
bull spinifex 26
bulrush 29
bumble, narrow-leaf 111
bunch panic 32
bush
  banana 124, 192, 197, 198
  bean 197
  coconut 170
  potato 189, 198
  tomato 71, 72, 99
bush tomato, banana-
    flavoured 73
  bony-fruited 77
  clay-soil 76
  dog-eye 77
  grey 74
butterfly bush 140
button grass 18

cabbage palm 180
Calandrinia balonensis 38
Callitris glaucophylla 162
Calocephalus platycephalus 58
Canthium attenuatum 108
  latifolium 108
  lineare 109
caper bush 113
Capparis lasiantha 110
  loranthifolia 111, 117
  mitchellii 112, 114
  spinosa var. *nummularia*
    113, 117
  umbonata 114
Carissa lanceolata 115
cassia, desert 145
cassias 144, 201
caterpillar, tar vine 37
caterpillars 131, 176 (*and see*

  grubs [edible])
cattail 29
caustic vine 143
  weed 43
Celerio lineata livornicoides 37
Centipeda minima 39
  thespidioides 39
chocolate bush 146
Choiromyces aboriginum 203
Chrysocephalum
  apiculatum 58
  semicalvum 58
citrus, native 108
clay-soil bush tomato 76
claypan samphire 78
Cleome viscosa 40
Clerodendrum floribundrum
  116
coconut, bush 170
Codonocarpus cotinifolius 125,
  136
colony wattle 102
conkleberry (conkerberry)
  115
coolibah 166
corkwood, fork-leafed 178
  long-leafed 178
  northern 177, 179
Corymbia aparrerinja 174, 201
  opaca 170
Crinum flaccidum 41
Crotalaria cunninghamii 64
crumbweed, green 42
cucumber, native 188, 195
Cucumis melo ssp. *agrestis*
  188, 195
cumbungi 29
currant, native 108
curly windmill grass 19
cycad palm 181
Cymbopogon ambiguus 16
Cynanchum floribundum 126
Cyperus bulbosus 17

Dactyloctenium radulans 18
daisybush, salt 68

daisy, Tietkins **58**
dead finish **105**
desert
  amaranthus **35**
  bloodwood **122, 170**
  cassia **145**
  fig *100*, **175**
  Flinders grass **32**, *94*
  heliotropes **45**
  kurrajong **161**
  lantern **34**
  mulga **101, 148**
  oak **159**
  poplar **125**
  raisin **70**, *98*
  sedge **22**
  thryptomene **147**
  truffle **203**
  yam **189, 198**
Dodonaea ssp. *mucronata* **127**
  viscosa ssp. *angustissima* **127**
dog-eye bush tomato **77**
dogwood **154**
dogwood hakea **179**
Duboisia hopwoodii **128, 141**
dwarf bird flower **64**
Dysphania kalpari **42**
  rhadinostachya **42**
Elderia arenivaga **203**
elegant acacia **107**, *121*
emu bush **131**, *118*
emu poison bush **128**
Enchylaena tomentosa **65**
Enteropogon acicularis **19**
  ramosus **19**
Eragrostis dielsii **21**
  eriopoda **20, 21, 23**
  falcata **21**
  leptocarpa **21**
  setifolia **21**
Eremophila duttonii **129**
  freelingii **100, 130**
  longifolia **131**, *118*
Erythrina vespertilio **163**
Eucalyptus camaldulensis var. *obtusa* **122, 164**

Eucalyptus
  chippendalei **171**
  coolabah ssp. *arida* **166**
  eucentrica **167**
  gamophylla **168**
  leucophloia **169**
  opaca *122*, **170**
  oxymitra **172**
  pachyphylla **173**
  papuana **174, 201**
  sessilis **173**
  socialis (*see* E. eucentrica)
  victrix **166**
Euphorbia drummondii **43**

Ficus species **202**
Ficus platypoda var. *minor* *100*, **175**
fig, desert *100*, **175**
  wild *100*, **175**
Fimbristylis eremophila **22**
  oxystachya **22**
fire wattle **86**
firebush **146**
flat-leaved hakea **179**
Flinders grass, desert **32**, *94*
fork-leafed corkwood **178**
fuchsia, hill *100*, **130**

gall, bloodwood **170**
georgina gidgee **156**
ghost gum **174, 201**
gidgee, black **158**
  georgina **156**
  myall **153**
gidgee wild orange **111**
Gnaphalium luteo-album **58**
Gomphrena species **58**
Goodenia lunata **44**
gooseberry, native **188, 195**
  wild **75**
goosefoot, rat-tail **42**
grass, porcupine **24, 25**
grass tree **148**
green crumbweed **42**

Grevillea species **135**, 201
Grevillea eriostachya **132**, *119*
   juncifolia 132, *119*, **133**, 134, 176
   nematophylla 135
   pterosperma 135
   stenobotrya **134**
   striata **176**
   wickhamii ssp. *aprica* **135**
grevillea, bird-flower 132, *119*
   holly leaf **135**
   honey 132, *119*, **133**, 134, 176
   rattlepod **134**
   sandhill **134**
grey bush tomato **74**
grub, witchetty 19, **88**, *120*, 160
   yeperenye (yipirinya) **37**
grubs (edible) 59, 69, 83, 91, 92, 102, 106, 107 125, 131, 144, 145, 146, 156, 160, 161, 163, **164**, 165, 166, **170**, 174
gum, ghost **174**, 201
   snappy **169**
Gyrostemon ramulosus **136**
   tepperi **136**

Hakea species 135, 201
Hakea chordophylla **177**, 179
   divaricata **178**
   leucoptera 118, **137**
   macrocarpa **179**
   suberea 177, **178**
hakea, dogwood **179**
   flat-leaved **179**
handflower, heavy-soil **44**
   tobacco **44**
hard spinifex 24, **25**, 26
hawkmoth 37
headache vine **194**
heavy-soil handflower **44**
heliotropes, desert **45**
Heliotropium asperrimum **45**
   cunninghamii 45
   tenuifolium (line illustration) 45
Helipterum tietkensii (see *Rhodanthe tietkensii*)
hepialid moth (larva) 165
hill
   fuchsia **100**, **130**
   mulga **157**
holly leaf grevillea **135**
honey 66, 83, 132, 133, 135, 147, 151, **164**, 165, 167, 168, 171, 172, 173, 174, 177, 178, 179
honey grevillea 132, *119*, **133**, 134, 176
honey(dew) 151, 155
hop bush **127**
horse mulga **103**

Ipomoea costata 123, **189**, 191, 198
   muelleri **191**
ironwood 155
Isotoma petraea **46**
isotome, rock **46**

kangaroo balls vine **195**
keeled lantern bush **34**
kino **170**, 176
kurapuka **104**
kurrajong, desert **161**
kurumaru **136**

lamb's tail **57**
lantern, desert **34**
lantern bush, keeled **34**
leather-leaved colony wattle **106**
lemon grass, native **16**
Lepidium muelleri-ferdinandi **47**
   oxytrichum 47
   phlebopetalum 47
Leptosema chambersii **66**

lerp scales 83, 87, *122*, **151**, 155, 158, **165**, 166, 171, 172, 173
Leschenaultia divaricata 67
leschenaultia, tangled 67
life-saver burr 60
lily, Sandover 41
Livistona mariae 180
long-leafed corkwood 178
love grasses 21
lukarrara 22
Lysiana species **200 ff.**
Lysiana exocarpi ssp. *exocarpi* 202
   murrayi 200, **202**
   spathulata 202
   subfalcata 202

Macrozamia macdonnellii 181
mallee, blue 168
   red **167**, 173
   round-fruited 172
   water 167
Marsdenia australis 124, **192**, 197
mat spurge 43
Melaleuca species 202
Melaleuca bracteata 139
   dissitiflora 139
   fulgens ssp. *corrugata* 139
   glomerata **138**, 139
   lasiandra 139
   trichostachya 139
melon, native **188**, 195
   ulcardo **188**, 195
milk weed 43
millet, armgrass 30
   native 23, *94*
millionaire's cabbage 180
mimosa bush 85
mint bush *100*, **141**
mistletoe **200 ff.**
morning glory, native **191**
Mukia maderaspatana **194**
   sp. *c* (*M.* A50961 Glen Helen Station) **195**

mulga 87, *121*, **150**, 201
mulga, desert **101**, 148
   hill **157**
   horse **103**
mulga: associated foods 151
mulga
   apple **152**
   bean **197**
   native currant **109**
mulla-mulla 57
mungilypa 78
munyeroo 55
mustard grass 47
myall, northern **153**
myall gidgee **153**
Mycocleandia arenacea **203**
   bulundari **203**
Myriocephalus stuartii 58

nalgoo 17
narrow-leaf bumble **111**
narrow-leaved native currant **109**
native
   bees 19, **165**, 166, 171, 185
   citrus **108**
   cucumber **188**, 195
   currant **108**
   gooseberry **188**, 195
   lemon grass **16**
   melon **188**, 195
   millet 23, *94*
   morning glory **191**
   peach **183**
   pear **126**
   pine **162**
   tomato 75
   truffle **203**
   watercress 47
   willow **182**
native currant, mulga **109**
   narrow-leaved **109**
native tobacco, round-leaved 50
   shiny-leaved **51**, *97*
needle bush **137**

needlewood *118*, **137**
Nicotiana species 44, **48 ff.**, 54
    (see also pituri)
Nicotiana benthamiana **50**
    excelsior **51**, *97*
    gossei 51, **52**, *97*
    megalosiphon 54
    occidentalis 54
    rosulata ssp. *ingulba* **53**
    simulans 54
    velutina 54
northern
    corkwood **177**, *179*
    myall **153**
    wild orange **114**

oak, desert **159**
odd-leaf wattle **86**
oilgrass, scented **16**
Onchrogaster species 176
onion grass **17**
orange, wild **112**

palm, cabbage **180**
    cycad **181**
Palm Valley palm **180**
Pandorea doratoxylon **196**
Panicum decompositum **23**, *94*
paperbark **138**, *139*
parakeelya **38**
parrot plant **64**
passionfruit, wild **113**, *117*
peach, native **183**
peach tree **183**
pear, native **126**
    silky **192**, *197*
pencil wattle **103**
    yam *123*, **199**
Petalostylis cassioides **140**
pigweed **55**
pine, native **162**
pintye-pintye **61**
pirraru **82**
Pittosporum phylliraeoides **182**

pituri (and pituri substitutes)
    44, **48 ff.**, 75, 116, 128,
    138, 176
pituri, ash for 89, 134, 144,
    151, 153, 154, 155, 158,
    159, 165, 166, 185
    rock **52**, *97*
    rubbish 54
    sandhill 53
pituri bush **128**, 141
Plectrachne species *(see*
    Triodia)
Pluchea ferdinandi-muelleri **68**
    dunlopii **68**
plum, wild **141**
plum bush **141**
Podaxis pistillaris **124**, **204**
poison bush, emu **128**
poplar, desert **125**
porcupine grass **24**, **25**
Portulaca oleracea **55**
potato, bush **189**, **198**
potato bush **75**
poverty bush, red **121**
Prostanthera striatiflora **100**,
    141
Psylla eucalypti **165**
Pterocaulon serrulatum **56**, *95*
    sphacelatum **56**
Ptilotus species **57**
Ptilotus exaltatus **57**
    obovatus **69**
    sessifolius 69
puffball, stalked **124**, **204**
purslane **55**
pussytails **57**
Pycnoporus coccineus **205**

quandong *121*, **183**

raisin, desert **70**, *98*
rat-tail goosefoot **42**
rattlepod, sandhill **64**
rattlepod grevillea **134**
red gum, river *122*, **164**
red mallee **167**, **173**

red poverty bush **121**
resin 24, 27 ff., 67, 101, 148, 156, 158, 162, **170**, 171, 174, 176
Rhodanthe tietkensii **58**
Rhyncharrhena linearis **197**
river red gum *122*, **164**
summer grass **31**
rock isotome **46**
pituri **52**, *97*
rolypoly **59**
round-fruited mallee **172**
round-leaved native tobacco **50**
rubbish pituri **54**
ruby saltbush **65**

Salsola kali **59**
salt daisybush **68**
saltbush, ruby **65**
samphire, claypan **78**
sand sunray **58**
sand-bush, soft-leaved **136**
sandhill grevillea **134**
pituri **53**
rattlepod **64**
teatree **139**
Sandover lily **41**
Santalum acuminatum 121, **183**
lanceolatum **142**
Sarcostemma viminale ssp. *australe* **143**
scarlet bracket fungus **205**
scented oilgrass **16**
scent grass **16**
scrub wattle **104**
sedge, desert **22**
Senna artemisioides ssp. **144**
ssp. *artemisioides* **145**
ssp. *filifolia* **145**
ssp. *helmsii* **144**
ssp. *oligophylla* **144**
Senna pleurocarpa **146**
shiny-leaved native tobacco **51**, *97*

wattle **82**
sickle-leaved wattles **83**
Sida platycalyx **60**
silky pear **192**, 197
silver witchetty **84**
smoke bush **69**
smooth spiderbush **116**
snake vine **198**
snappy gum **169**
sneeze weeds **39**
soft spinifex 24, 27
soft-leaved sand-bush **136**
Solanum centrale **70**, *98*
chippendalei **71**, 72, *99*
cleistogamum **73**
coactiliferum **74**
diversiflorum **72**
ellipticum **75**, 77
esuriale **76**
petrophilum **77**
quadriloculatum **77**
spearwood (spearbush) **196**
spiderbush, smooth **116**
spinifex **24 ff.**
spinifex, buck 25, **26**
bull **26**
hard 24, 25, **26**
soft 24, **27**
spiny-leaved wattle **91**
split-jack **110**
stalked puffball *124*, **204**
Stemodia viscosa **61**, *95*
stiff wattle **91**
Stuart's pea **64**
sugarbag 19, 171, 185
summer grass **30**
summer grass, river **31**
sunray, sand **58**
suplejack (supplejack) **185**
sweet pillow **61**

tangled leschenaultia **67**
tar vine **36**
tar vine caterpillar **37**
teatree **138**, 139
teatree, sandhill **139**

Tecticornia verrucosa **78**
teddy bear's arsehole **60**
thryptomene, desert **147**
Thryptomene maisonneuvii **147**
tickweed **40**
Tietkins daisy **58**
Tinospora smilacina **198**
tobacco, wild **48**
tobacco handflower **44**
tomato, bush **71**, **72**, *99*
   native **75**
Trictena argentata 165
Trigona species 171
Triodia species **24 ff.**, 67, 148
Triodia basedowii **25**
   longiceps 25, **26**
   pungens 24, 25, 26, **27**, *93*, 101
truffle, desert (native) **203**
tumbleweed **59**
turpentine bush **90**
Typha domingensis **29**

ulcardo melon **188**, 195
umbrella bush **89**
upside-down plant **66**
Urochloa piligera **30**, 31
   praetervisa **30**

velvet hill wattle **80**
Ventilago viminalis **185**
Vigna lanceolata 123, **199**

water mallee **167**
watercress, native **47**
wattle, blue **106**
   colony **102**
   fire **86**
   leather-leaved colony **106**
   odd-leaf **86**
   pencil **103**
   scrub **104**
   shiny-leaved **82**
   sickle-leaved **83**
   spiny-leaved **91**
   stiff **91**
   velvet hill **80**
   waxy **92**
   whipstick **81**
waxy wattle **92**
whipstick wattle **81**
whitewood **160**
wild
   fig *100*, **175**
   gooseberry **75**
   orange **112**
   orange, gidgee **111**
   orange, northern **114**
   passionfruit **113**, *117*
   plum **141**
   tobacco **48**
willow, native **182**
windmill grass, curly **19**
wire bush **67**
witchetty, silver **84**
witchetty bush **87**, *120*, 201
   grub 19, **88**, *120*, 160
woollybutt **20**

Xanthorrhea thorntonii **148**
Xyleutes biarpiti **88**, *120*

Yakirra australiensis **32**, *94*
yalka **17**
yam, desert **189**, 198
   pencil *123*, **199**
yeperenye (yipirinya) grub **37**

NOTES

NOTES

NOTES

NOTES